GOAL!

THE ART OF
SCORING

GOAL!
THE ART OF SCORING

JASON TOMAS

highdown

Published in 2004 by Highdown,
an imprint of Raceform Ltd
Compton, Newbury, Berkshire, RG20 6NL
Raceform Ltd is a wholly-owned subsidiary of Trinity Mirror plc

A CIP catalogue record for this book is available from the British Library.

ISBN 1-904317-72-3

Designed by Fiona Pike
Printed in Great Britain by William Clowes Ltd, Beccles, Suffolk

Dedication

To Isabella

CONTENTS

INTRODUCTION

Malcolm Macdonald
has a lot to answer for.

Goalscoring is a subject that has intrigued me for some time. But if anybody has been responsible for turning this into an insatiable hunger for knowledge about the art – and, indeed, pushing me down the road leading to this book – it is Macdonald.

As a football journalist I had the pleasure of spending a great deal of time in the former Newcastle, Arsenal and England centre-forward's company when he was manager of Fulham in the early 1980s. What made it so stimulating was that, in our conversations about strikers and how they operated, Macdonald gave deeper and more perceptive insights into the subject than any of the other scorers or ex-scorers I had spoken to.

Macdonald's first-team coach then was Ray Harford, and when Harford worked with Alan Shearer at Blackburn in the 1990s, his willingness to improve my appreciation of the secrets behind the striker's success – beyond those that were already well-known on a superficial level – was another factor which helped bring about the birth of this book.

There is, indeed, much more to consistently putting the ball in the net than often meets the eye. There are so many strands to the subject and, even now, it is difficult to escape the nagging feeling that it might take more than one book for me to rid myself of that hunger for goal knowledge for good. As I said, Malcolm Macdonald has a lot to answer for.

However, this is not meant as a textbook on the subject. Rather it is a documentary, concentrating on the contemporary game, which sets out to both inform and entertain.

In my quest to shed more light on the art of scoring, I am indebted to the 'service' I have received from a number of 'team-mates'. I am particularly indebted to the figures who were happy to give me the benefit of their expert knowledge – notably (in alphabetical order) Ade Akinbyi, John Aldridge, Steve Archibald, James Beattie, Bill Beswick, Craig Brown, Ray Clarke, Ray Clemence, Mervyn Day, Dion Dublin, Paul Elliott, Trevor Francis, David Healy, Mark McGhee, Gary Pallister, Kevin Phillips, David Pleat, Bryan 'Pop' Robson, Steve Round, Andy Roxburgh, Graeme Sharp, Alan Shearer, Gordon Smith, Gordon Strachan, Paul Sturrock, John Syer and Gordon Wallace.

My thanks, also, to Alex Norman and Jamie Jackson for their research help, to Simon Wilson at ProZone, and to Patrick Barclay, Alex Fynn, David Luxton and, of course, to my publisher Jonathan Taylor, for their moral support.

Jason Tomas
June 2004

CHAPTER ONE
BURNING UP THE FIELD

'The best strikers are the ones
who prompt opposing defences
to change their normal style of play,
and usually the strikers who come
into that category are the ones
who are the quickest …
The last thing a defender wants
to see is a striker's backside.'
GARY PALLISTER

For every footballer, at any level, nothing can compare with the buzz of scoring a goal. Some have claimed that it is even better than sex. During a BBC Radio 5 Live programme on goalscoring in January 2004, Dr Mark Hamilton, Radio One's 'resident Sunday Surgery physician', was happy to expand on the analogy. 'They say that sex is broken down into three main parts, desire, stimulation [the build-up play?] and the climax at the end, which is putting the ball in the back of the net.' When strikers have done that, he added, 'they are kind of drunk on their own body's chemicals'.

But one does not need to put the ball in the net to experience this. The colleagues of the goalscorers – managers, coaches and team-mates – seem to get just as much excitement out of watching them do it. Of course, as goals are the most important aspect of the game, the whole point of the game, the same applies to the vast majority of the millions of people who follow it.

Indeed, it says much about the stimulating effect of seeing that ball nestling in the net that Fifa, the governing body of world football, cannot seem to get enough of it. Since the football laws were initially formulated in 1863, almost all of of Fifa's numerous changes to the rules, or their instructions to referees on the interpretation of them, have been designed to produce more goals. On top of the major recent amendments relating to such scoring obstacles as offside and the tackle from behind, Fifa have even attempted to make the goals bigger, on the grounds that the average heights of the men guarding them have increased since the present dimensions – eight yards by eight feet – were set in the 1800s.

How today's strikers would love to have been around before then, in the days when football and rugby were evolving in public schools and goals were all manner of different shapes and sizes. Eton's was eleven feet wide and seven feet tall; Uppingham's, though only five feet tall, ran the entire width of the pitch. In 1863, the schools and colleges reached agreement on a standard goal comprising two poles eight yards apart but with no upper limit. The standardised height of eight feet was set in 1865.

According to the head of Fifa, Sepp Blatter, the goals should be lengthened by the diameter of two balls (about 50cm) and the height by the diameter of one. But what he seemed to overlook, apart from the probability that such a change would lead to more rather than less defensive football, was the extent to which the basic tools of the players' trade – the balls and boots – have altered.

Because of the developments in the materials and design of their playing equipment, players generally can now hit shots with greater power and accuracy than ever before. In some matches the balls have seemed more like the ones one might find on a beach, the players apparently able to make them do almost everything but sing and dance. Goalkeepers might have been made to look like dummies, but the trend for the dice to be loaded in favour of attacking players generally, and goalscorers particularly, is one that Fifa and the public have welcomed.

The fact is, though, that scoring, on a regular basis over a long period, has always been an elusive art, and it always will be. If anything, it could be argued that consistent scoring has become harder. Defenders now are fitter and more athletic, and they get more help from other members of their teams. In addition, the increasingly vast sums of money at stake have prompted teams generally to be more concerned about avoiding defeat than about winning. At club level, perhaps only Real Madrid, who have had a greater number of outstanding attacking players than any other team in the world, have consistently performed without any fears about conceding goals, though even Real were moved to agree that a change of attitude was necessary when they lost to Monaco in the 2003/04 European Championship League semi-final – after establishing a 5-2 lead – and finished fourth in La Liga.

As we saw in the European Championship in Portugal, the more important the match, the 'tighter' it is liable to be. Therefore, the more important the match, the greater the pressure on the players with the major responsibility for breaking the deadlock. 'At one time I thought about it so much beforehand that I felt knackered even before the start of a game,' Southampton's Kevin Phillips said. 'I'd analyse things to the point where by the time I was ready to take the field I had confused myself. My brain was so full of information and various thoughts about how I might score that I ended up not knowing what to do. I have spoken to a lot of strikers about this, and they have had the same experiences. I have learnt to relax more as I have got older, but after a game my mind is racing so much that no matter how physically tired I am I still have difficulty in getting to sleep. It's not so bad after a match on a Saturday – like everybody else at the weekend, you can unwind by going out and having a few drinks – but after a midweek match, when you have to be more careful about this, I usually can't get to sleep until three or four in the morning.'

Steve Archibald, the former Aberdeen, Tottenham and

Barcelona striker, added, 'All players like to score goals, but if they are not strikers, they are more or less just playing at it. It's kid's stuff compared to what the real goalscorers have to go through.' And the demand for these men exceeds the supply. Thus, the leading scorers or goal creators have tended to command the highest transfer fees; they are also the figures who tend to earn the most money and attract the most publicity. At the start of the 2003/04 season, the only defender among the ten worldwide players to have had the highest fees paid for them was Rio Ferdinand, who in 2002 cost Manchester United a British record £30 million. Ferdinand was also the only defender among the ten highest earners. Still, after the 2004 European Championship in Portugal, it seemed only a matter of time before Ferdinand would be usurped by an 18-year-old striker – Wayne Rooney, of course.

But one does not need to be in the class of Rooney, Thierry Henry, Ruud van Nistelrooy and Michael Owen – the ultimate love gods, as Dr Mark Hamilton might describe such figures – to make players in other positions jealous. Stoke City's Ade Akinbiyi, one of the less fêted members of the strikers' union, put it this way: 'Strikers are in a stronger position career-wise than most other players. Once you have established a reasonable record as a goalscorer you will always find clubs willing to take a chance on you.' So the message for the proverbial Mrs Worthington is clear: it might not be a good idea to put her daughter on the stage, but if she has a son, and he's a goalscorer, the football stage is a different matter entirely.

What are the attributes she should look for in him? What are the qualities that separate the great strikers from the good, average or comparatively impotent ones? Even for a man as knowledgeable on the subject as Andy Roxburgh, the technical director of Uefa (the European football governing body), such questions can easily cause a headache. 'It's difficult to know where to begin,' said Roxburgh, a former striker who was Scotland's coach before taking up his Uefa post. 'It's a very complex web of things. To start with, I think you have to make a distinction between a finisher – and a finisher to me is someone who literally just finishes an attacking move with one or two touches – and the artist, who involves himself in the build-up play and creates his own chances. Two players I worked with in the Scotland squad who were in the latter category were Charlie Nicholas and Kenny Dalglish. Both were able to get goals in situations where no obvious chance existed. In today's game, Thierry Henry is a wonderful example of a player who combines the creation of a chance with the taking of it, whereas people such as Alan Shearer are magnificent finishers.'

Strikers, indeed, come in all shapes and sizes, and not just in their builds. Some are especially good in the air whereas others give the impression of having been influenced by that medical opinion about heading causing brain damage. On the ground, they can also be split into different categories in relation to their pace.

Generally, strikers who are exceptionally quick are the ones who can be seen bursting into the space behind opposing defences, either taking the ball into those positions themselves or chasing passes into them, while those who are relatively slow are more liable to receive the ball to their feet, with their backs to the goal. Many of the outstanding post-war scoring partnerships in England have featured both types. It is no coincidence that the players with the most pace, or more specifically an outstanding change of pace, tend best to mirror Roxburgh's point about strikers creating goals on their own. 'These are the ones who can deal with having a big space between them and the goal,' he explained. 'That is what Michael Owen is good at. Give him the ball thirty or forty yards from goal with two or three defenders in front of him, and if he has a clear run at them, they are dead.'

One of Owen's England managers, Glenn Hoddle, might have expressed doubts about whether he was as 'natural' a finisher as counterparts like Robbie Fowler, but even Hoddle could not help but applaud Owen for the way he propelled himself into scoring positions. 'I don't think I have seen many regular scorers who are able to attack defenders with the ball like Michael does,' he once said. 'Normally you find that in wingers like Ryan Giggs rather than in out-and-out strikers. A lot of players are quick movers but not so quick with the ball at their feet.' Who can ever forget the Owen goal against Argentina in the 1998 World Cup finals in France, when he sprinted past Jose Chamot and Roberto Ayala with the ball before angling a right-foot shot into the left corner of the net? And who can forget his hat-trick, and the part his pace played generally, in England's astonishing 5–1 victory over Germany in Munich in September 2001?

Roxburgh himself, while readily conceding that he was more of a 'finisher' than an 'artist' (and no more than a middle-of-the-road Scottish league finisher at that), had plenty of pace. It was certainly helpful to him when he operated up front with Alex Ferguson at Falkirk, with Fergie the target man and Roxburgh feeding off him. 'Generally, strikers are quicker than back-line guys, but that was particularly the case when I was a player,' Roxburgh said. 'If it was a straight run, I could beat most defenders – indeed, most of my goals came from through-passes, shots on the run. I don't think I was tough or strong enough, or had a good enough touch, to be more than what I was. But thanks to my pace and finishing, I didn't have a bad career.'

Among others who confirm the advantages of such attributes is Trevor Francis. Quite apart from how they helped him to establish an outstanding career as a striker, Francis recalled the case of one of the players he worked with when he was Sheffield Wednesday's manager, Paul Warhurst. Though Warhurst was a centre-half, his switch to a striking role by Francis in the 1992/93 season was so successful that, as Francis said, 'He probably made a bigger impact as a front player than any of the more natural strikers I worked with. At Wednesday, I had lost my regular strikers through injury, notably David Hirst, and felt that Paul might do a stop-gap job for me because he was so quick and was a good striker of the ball. I have always liked to see plenty of pace in forwards. I think most defenders will tell you that pace, properly applied, is the most difficult quality for them to counter. Paul had fantastic pace, and when we played him as a striker in the first team his impact was remarkable. I don't think he had ever operated in that role before in senior professional football, but if you hadn't known who he was you would have sworn that he was a natural centre-forward. Indeed, there was even speculation that Graham Taylor [then England manager] might pick him as a striker for the national team.'

Warhurst was particularly effective in the cup competitions, helping Wednesday reach the finals of both the League Cup and FA Cup (both lost against Arsenal) with a total of nine goals in twelve ties. Eventually he and Francis fell out, ironically over the latter's decision to switch him back to the heart of the defence for the FA Cup final and the replay, and four months later he sold Warhurst to Blackburn. 'Wednesday had paid £750,000 for Paul [from Oldham in July 1991],' said Francis, 'but because of his success with us as a striker that season, we got £2.7 million for him.'

As for what being exceptionally quick did for Francis as a striker, he'll remind you of his initial success in a struggling team at Birmingham City. Francis, who made his Birmingham debut at the age of sixteen and went on to score 128 goals for the club before Nottingham Forest made him Britain's first £1 million player in 1979, has mixed feelings about the view that his record at St Andrews would have been even more impressive in a better side. In a way, he argued, his pace made Birmingham City perfect for him. 'We were often under pressure, especially away from home, but these were the periods when I felt I had my best chance of scoring. OK, over a season I would have got more chances in a team like Liverpool than I did with Birmingham. But equally, with the opposition dominating the game and pushing forward against us, I knew that I would always get the chance to use my pace on the break.'

Some strikers are quicker than they look. Ruud van Nistelrooy has suggested that this is an aspect of his game that tends to be underestimated. In a *Sunday Times* interview in April 2003 it was revealed that the only Manchester United players faster than the Dutchman were Giggs and Mikael Silvestre. Referring to his running style, though, he said, 'You see Thierry [Henry] and it's beautiful. You see me, it's not classic. It is a little bit the same with Robert Pires: he does not pick his knees up. I've worked on it, trying to get more quickness in my feet, more power. It changes. Sometimes I see myself and I think, "Now it looks nice."'

Certainly when the jet-heeled Henry is in full flow it looks little short of awesome. During the 2003/04 season, the most vivid illustration of a striker exploiting his acceleration was Henry's 'wonder goal' in Arsenal's 5–1 European Champions League win over Inter Milan in Italy. The Italians, having had a penalty appeal rejected, were caught stretched at the back as Henry burst forward with the ball. The Inter defender Javier Zanetti, the only outfield player between Henry and the goal, did well to hold him up; indeed, with Zanetti keeping two or three yards in front of him, Henry stopped, as if caught in two minds about whether to take him on or wait for support. Few would have bet on his doing the former, given the ground he had to make up in order to beat Zanetti and the fact that other Milan players were getting into covering positions around him. But take him on he did. A marvellous double dummy by Henry was followed by an explosive burst that took him past Zanetti as if the Argentinian was wearing diving boots; and, finally, a wonderful shot into the far corner of the net.

It is that physical explosiveness that also characterises AC Milan's Andriy Shevchenko, another member of the European super striker pack. 'No striker in the world is more dangerous on the break than Shevchenko,' Roxburgh said. 'At his previous club, Dynamo Kiev, he worked twice a day on speed endurance, and in fact when he was transferred to AC Milan [in 1999] it was felt that he would not train the same way in Italy and would deteriorate as a result.' But in a football environment recognised as the hardest in the world for strikers, the Ukrainian speed machine has repeatedly been among the leading scorers. During the 2003/04 season, when he finished top of the Serie A scorers' list for the second time with 24, it was difficult to imagine any fans in the world not dreaming of seeing him in their team's line-up. His most ardent admirers included Chelsea's mega-rich new Russian owner Roman Abramovic, a close friend of Shevchenko. This was reflected by a tabloid report that Abramovic was prepared to pay the Italian club as much as £80 million for him – almost double the world-record transfer fee that Real Madrid paid Juventus for Zinedine Zidane in 2001.

It is of course more than just pace that makes the Shevchenko types such valuable commodities. Nonetheless, in any survey to find the most valuable asset for a striker, fleet-footedness would unquestionably be at the top of the list. One reason why all strikers dream of being able to cover the ground like Olympic sprinters is the dilemma it creates for opposing teams in deciding how far their defenders can push forward to compress the play and how tightly defenders can afford to mark them. Providing the strikers are able to time their runs well enough to avoid being caught offside – an art for which Gary Lineker was particularly noted – the teams facing them are always liable to be neurotic about leaving a lot of space behind their back lines. But reducing the space between the back-four players and the goalkeeper creates another potential problem, that of strikers being able to exploit the extra space in front of the defence by getting a run at them with the ball.

'The best strikers are the ones who prompt opposing defences to change their normal style of play, and usually the strikers who come into that category are the ones who are the quickest,' said Gary Pallister, the former Middlesbrough, Manchester United and England defender. 'If you are playing against a striker who is not going to outrun you, or is at his best in the air, then you push up and keep him as far from the goal as you can. It's different with the exceptionally quick strikers: generally, I would say that attempting to force them to play in front of you is a much better option than giving them the scope to get behind you. The last thing a defender wants to see is a striker's backside.'

'From a striker's point of view,' said Trevor Francis, 'a lot depends not just on the timing of his runs but also on his getting the ball played to him early. If I had been the manager of a team with someone like me in it, I would not have wanted a particularly slow build-up. It also helps to have players behind you who can see a pass and implement it. This was something I really appreciated when I played in Italy [for Sampdoria] with Ray Wilkins and then Graeme Souness. As they gained control, I would come towards the ball, with my defender following me, knowing full well that if it was "on" for the ball to be played into the space behind for me to run on to it they would immediately recognise this and act on it. But it is important to be able to vary things. If I came off the defender and he wasn't going to give me that space in behind – he was going to allow me to get the ball to my feet – well, that was a great situation for me, too. I don't think anything was better for me than a one-against-one situation with a defender because I could run faster with the ball than most other players, and I could also go either side. Provided you come off the defender properly – come off at an angle, half-turned [to increase the angle of vision] rather than square on – and you have good control, you are the governor then.

'I could name a lot of present-day players who emphasise these points. But the one who comes into my mind straight away is Michael Owen. He reminds me so much of myself.'

Gary Pallister was among the quickest central defenders, but even he could be made to look slow. Indeed, discussions about the advantages for strikers in being able to run faster than their markers immediately led him to his experiences against Romario, when the Brazilian was playing for Barcelona, and Henry.

Pallister faced Romario during Manchester United's two European Champions League matches in the 1994/95 season, and he admits that the memories of them still cause him to 'cringe with embarrassment'.

For the first match at Old Trafford, Alex Ferguson was so concerned about Romario's pace that he left Steve Bruce, United's captain and Pallister's central defensive partner, out of the team and brought in Paul Parker to do a man-for-man marking job against the striker. The change in tactics bothered Pallister, who felt that United would have been better off sticking to the zonal defensive system to which they were accustomed. 'Steve Bruce and I always felt this,' he said. 'For example, whenever we played against Niall Quinn [Sunderland], the fact that I was as tall as him would cause the gaffer to give me the responsibility of marking him. But Steve and I felt there were situations in which I should leave him, that it was much more important for us to keep our defensive shape.' If any match influenced Pallister's views on this, it was England's 2–0 defeat by

Norway in the World Cup qualifying tie in Oslo in June 1993. Pallister had been brought back into the side by manager Graham Taylor to do a man-marking job on Jostein Flo. 'I was more or less trying to track him all over the place at times and it unbalanced the whole team,' he said.

Hence the fact that, while he did not go so far as to tell Parker to ignore Ferguson's instructions for that home match against Barcelona, Pallister did suggest that he could occasionally afford to leave it to him to deal with Romario if the latter drifted into his area.

But there was some confusion between the two men when Romario broke clear onto a through-ball between Pallister and left-back Denis Irwin to make the score 1–1. Ferguson wrote in his autobiography, 'That goal angered me as my instruction had been for Parker to stay with Romario throughout. Our trouble had arisen because of the British custom of defending zones and our habit of passing the responsibility for dealing with an opposing attacker from one defender to another as the man enters a different area of the pitch. Big Gary Pallister had told Parker that he was ready to take care of Romario and then found that the Brazilian was leaving him stranded. What infuriated me was that we had spent three days adjusting our zonal defending method to incorporate man-for-man marking of Romario. I wouldn't have taken such pains if I didn't think the change was necessary.' The tie, which Ferguson felt United could and should have won, ended in a 2–2 draw. For his part, Pallister still has mixed feelings about the extent to which he might have been culpable. 'Though the gaffer gave me some stick about it [Romario's goal], I still feel that in the long run it [the zonal approach] was the better way to go about things.'

Pallister was even more uncomfortable during United's 4–0 defeat in the return tie when their defence, not helped by the gung-ho attacking boldness of some of their colleagues in front of them, was repeatedly tormented by Romario and his Bulgarian striking partner Hristo Stoichkov. 'They tore us apart with their pace and movement,' he recalled. 'I just could not live with Romario. It was the only time I have walked off the park after a defeat with no answers. I will always remember Romario's goal. When he came off the front and turned, I was maybe two or three yards in front of him. I knew he was going to take me on and I thought, "Right, go on, let's see what you've got." The next second, he was past me. I was absolutely stunned.'

It was the same when Henry took Pallister to the cleaner's to score the only goal against Middlesbrough at the Riverside Stadium in November 2000. 'I would say that was probably my worst moment on a football field,' Pallister confessed. 'He is the quickest player I have ever come across. He looks sometimes as if he is just strolling through games, but when he knocks the ball past you he can make you look like the slowest player in the world. That is what happened in that match at Middlesbrough.

'It happens to all of us from time to time,' Pallister added, recalling how Des Walker – 'the quickest England defender by far when I was in the squad' – was 'blown away' by the pace of Holland's Marc Overmars in the World Cup qualifying tie at Wembley in 1993. That incident, which led to Walker bringing down Overmars in the penalty area and Holland converting the spot kick to get a 2–2 draw, signalled the end of the road for Walker as an England player. 'But he could not have felt worse than I did when Henry made me look a mug,' Pallister concluded.

There is an interesting similarity between Overmars and Henry in that both can be described as goalscoring left-wingers. Overmars, who once played with Henry at Arsenal, has always been a winger rather than a striker, whereas with Henry it has been the other way around since he joined Arsenal. Henry, a player of Caribbean parentage who was born and raised in a rundown suburb of Paris, scored plenty of goals as a boy, but because of his fleet-footedness and skill on the ball, and maybe also his slight build, the wing seemed the ideal spot for him in professional football. He was used as a left-winger or left-side attacking player at Monaco, where he was first subjected to the coaching and managerial abilities of Arsène Wenger, and it was in that position that he gained his World Cup winners' medal with France in 1998 (when he was their top scorer in the competition).

He was enjoying himself, but not after his £8 million move to Juventus in January 1999. The ultra-disciplined world of Serie A was hardly conducive to bringing out the best in a free attacking spirit like Henry. As he has said, 'We played 3–5–2 with me on the left [of the midfield group], and I had to cover the whole flank. I did my best for the team, but I had to make the choice all the time of whether to stay back and defend or go forward and attack. In the end it was too much of a problem for me. I'm not a defender and I had to leave.'

He had long wanted to join forces with Wenger again, at Arsenal. But when he finally got the chance to do so in September 1999, he did not expect Wenger to look upon him as a replacement for central striker Nicolas Anelka. 'If he had not suggested that I play through the middle I would never have thought of it,' he said. Arsenal had been forced to sell Anelka to Real Madrid because of the player's insistence on leaving the club. The blow was softened considerably by the £23 million transfer fee Real forked out for him – a remarkable return for the Gunners' original half a million investment in the Frenchman. But after Henry's opening appearances in Anelka's role, it was difficult to avoid the view that the £10.5 million Arsenal had paid for him was also well over the odds. He did not score in his opening 12 league matches, and at one point he was dropped. Looking back on those early months, in an interview with Match Magazine, Henry said, '[Playing as a striker] took a while to get used to again. When I was sixteen at Monaco I played as a striker, but when I got into the first team I had to play as a winger and started to lose confidence in front of goal. I had problems settling in England to begin with, and I think I missed more chances than I scored. All the time, Patrick Vieira [Arsenal's captain and his French World Cup colleague] used to tease me about it. At the beginning it was funny, but at the end it was true as well. And they weren't difficult chances, just a good shot for a normal striker, but sometimes I would shoot and it would end up by the clock at Highbury.'

Henry, struggling to adjust to the physical intensity of English football, admitted that he thought about asking Wenger to switch him back to the wing. But he didn't go through with it because of his faith in Wenger's ability to know what was best for him and the warmth and support he got from the Arsenal fans. 'When I had to come on the pitch they were always clapping me, and and when I used to miss a goal they were still singing,' he said. 'That's why I was still happy when I was not scoring. In Italy, if you miss a goal, even if you are [Gabriel] Batitusta or [Oliver] Bierhoff, they want to kill you. Here, they want to sing my name.'

This was particularly true when Henry scored his first Highbury goals in the 2–1 win over Derby County in November 1999. Arsenal had been a goal down at one stage, and Henry, whose only previous goal had been at Southampton in September, said: 'Those goals [both set up by Overmars] were my big turning point because they were typical striker's goals.' That season Henry ended up with a league total of seventeen, which put him sixth on the Premiership scoring list behind Kevin Phillips (Sunderland), Alan Shearer (Newcastle), Dwight Yorke, Andy Cole (both Manchester United) and Michael Bridges (Leeds). Since then, the only players to have finished a season ahead of him have been Jimmy Floyd Hasselbaink (Chelsea) in 2001 and van Nistelrooy in 2003. By the end of the 2003/04 season, his overall scoring record for Arsenal was 151 goals in 255 matches – just 34 short of the post-war club record established by Ian Wright over 288 matches. Some 112 of those goals had come in the Premiership, so another club record in Henry's sights was that of Cliff Bastin, the top Arsenal league scorer with 150 between 1929 and 1946.

As Bastin was also a left-winger, it is interesting to note that despite the change in Henry's job description he has continued to spend much of his time on the left flank. That has been his favourite starting position, as reflected by the number of goals he has scored with diagonal runs with the ball from that area and then shots with his right foot. All of which brings us back to Roxburgh's point about the problems speedy players can cause defences when they have plenty of running space. As Francis said, 'In effect, by coming from the left, Henry gives himself the full width of the field to work in.' This partly explains why Francis himself was initially used in a wide position, as a right-winger, when he joined Nottingham Forest. It was in that role, of course, that he scored Forest's goal in the 1–0 win over Malmö in the 1979 European Cup final.

An even better post-war comparison with Henry, perhaps, can be found in the case of George Best. Ask most people to name his role at Manchester United and they would almost certainly reply 'winger' rather than 'striker'. But look at his scoring record for United – 137 goals in 361 league matches and an overall total of 178 in 466 – and compare his goals-to-game ratio with that of United contemporaries such as Bobby Charlton and Denis Law. Charlton, who spent the early part of his United career on the left wing, was the highest scorer in the club's history with a grand total of 347 in 752 games; Law, the archetypal finisher, got 236 in 409 games.

The former Arsenal centre-half and captain Frank McLintock, one of the best defenders in England when Best was at his peak, said, 'When people ask me to name the best strikers I played against, the obvious choice would be Jimmy Greaves. But there would not be much in it between him and Best. I am sure a lot of people do not fully appreciate the number of goals Best scored. He got them with his right foot, his left foot, and he also got a fair number with his head. Whenever a player came at me from a deep position, my aim was always to force him on to his weaker foot, deny him the chance to attack me on either side. But you could not do that against Best. He glided at you like a snake, occasionally twisting and turning so much that you were almost falling on your backside. Henry is like that. Some forwards look as if they are busting a gut to get past you, but Henry – well, he makes it look so effortless, as if he has an extra gear.'

To a great extent, Best and Henry, through the areas they cover and their overall attacking flair, have transcended the guidelines by which most strikers are judged. In addition to Roxburgh's point about the distinction between 'finishers' and 'artists', this was driven home to me in my interviews with other scoring 'experts'. A number suggested that Henry belonged to a special category that almost necessitated a book of its own. One of the most common comments about the rivalry between Henry and van Nistelrooy, for example, is that the Dutchman's working area is smaller, narrower, and that he gets more close-range, straightforward goals. To many professionals, Henry is both a great scorer and a scorer of great goals (a description that can also be applied to Rooney), whereas van Nistelrooy is 'just' a great goalscorer.

On the subject of van Nistelrooy, Teddy Sheringham, among the most respected of all the Premiership strikers, has said, 'He is clinical. Chance–bang–goal. He doesn't get sloppy. When he's got two, he will put the third one in; when he's got three, he will want to get four. A lot of players get sloppy. He just wants to score goals. He is the classic striker.' Gary Pallister nodded in agreement. 'I think van Nistelrooy can punish you more. Henry can embarrass you with his pace and can get goals out of nothing, but van Nistelrooy picks up the little bits and pieces in and around the six-yard box more than he does.'

As if to emphasise his comment about the 'complexity' of the subject, Roxburgh provided further food for thought about scorers of the calibre of Henry, van Nistelrooy and Owen when he said, 'A bad player might have only one string to his bow, whereas a good player might have ten. I often liken it to the difference between the European Champions League coaches and the run-of-the mill ones. The top Champions League guys are obsessed with fine detail. It's the same with a striker. Obviously, the more options he has got, the harder he becomes to stop and the higher he can go.'

That logic is simple enough, but the extent to which strikers should broaden their abilities is a different matter altogether. Given the right team, some strikers can get away with being more 'predictable' than others. Roxburgh himself confirmed this with an anecdote about his own favourite striker, the former Real Madrid and Hungary player Ferenc Puskas. 'I once did an interview with Puskas at one of our [Uefa] coaching courses, in Budapest, and I asked him, "You were all left foot – why?" He made a joke of it. "Well," he replied, "I decided early on that you need at least one leg to stand and I decided it would be my right. There would have been no point in swinging my right foot at the ball because then I would have landed on my backside." Everybody laughed, but you could see what he was getting at. He was so good with that left foot that it wasn't necessary for him to use the right.' Roxburgh recalled that it was the same with Davie Cooper, the outside-left who played for

Clydebank when Roxburgh was a coach there and was later in Roxburgh's Scotland team. 'At Clydebank, we put him on the right flank to force him to use his right foot more. So what did he do? He just kept cutting inside and scoring with the left. He only scored one Scotland goal for me with the right, and that was a fluke, a miskick. It was a waste of time getting him to change because he did everything with that left foot, and he was brilliant at it.

'Strikers have to concentrate on what they are good at,' Roxburgh added. 'You look at crosses. When the ball came across for me, my natural instinct if it was chest high or lower was to lean away from the ball and try to volley it. I had done a lot of volleying practice as a boy and was very comfortable about connecting with the ball in that way. Now, in that situation, you will hear Andy Gray say on TV, "He should have put his head in there." It's not necessarily right. It's what Andy would have done – it's the way that Andy played – but other strikers are different.'

At the same time, it is difficult to quibble with Roxburgh's view about the advantages of strikers broadening their ability when one looks at Owen. Roxburgh drew attention to the second of the two late Owen goals that enabled Liverpool to beat Arsenal 2–1 in the 2001 FA Cup final. Both were scored with his 'weaker' left foot, and the second, following a stirring run on the left, was particularly uncharacteristic. 'Contrast this with his World Cup goal against Argentina [when Owen took the ball to his right and shot with his right foot across the keeper]. That had been the typical Michael Owen goal for as long as people could remember. But I know that during Gérard Houllier's time as Liverpool manager he spent a lot of time working with Michael on his left foot, and that both of them were thrilled with those goals against Arsenal because of this. Obviously, Michael is still going to score many more goals with his right foot than the left, but the improvement on his left side has made his "armoury" that much stronger. There have been other improvements in his game. Basically, I feel he has become shrewder, cleverer as he has got older.'

It was the same with Gary Lineker, who emerged from his spell at Barcelona a considerably more complete scorer than he had been at Leicester and Everton. It was the same, too, with Trevor Francis, which helps explain why he was in his late thirties when he finally pulled down the curtain on his league playing career. 'Had I not had to combine playing with managing, I would definitely have played on past the age of forty,' he said. 'The period I spent in Italy helped me enormously, because apart from the tremendous physical conditioning methods I became much more a student of the game there. My pace, my greatest attribute, had diminished, but what had not changed was my ability to control the ball, pass, cross and shoot. So as I got older I became a better footballer, a better goalscorer. In my first few months as QPR's player-manager [when he was 34], some of the goals I scored even prompted suggestions that I should be brought back into the England team.'

Of course, having plenty of strings to that scoring bow is what Henry has going for him too. When I asked Charlton's first-team coach, Mervyn Day, about the problems the Frenchman created for opposing teams during Arsenal's unbeaten 2003/04 Premiership campaign, he replied, 'Central defenders playing against Arsenal often find that they do not have someone to mark. Dennis Bergkamp, or whoever else operates up front with Henry, drops short, while Henry likes to come down the left side. You know that Henry, with his phenomenal pace, is always liable to cut inside, on to his right foot, so in our matches against Arsenal we would be inclined to flood that area. Our right-back would be told not to go forward, not even if somebody on the other side was going down the other flank and was looking for a player to get on the end of a cross to the far post, and our right-side midfielder would probably have to hold back as well.' In the light of this, it is interesting to note that Henry scored the equaliser in the 1–1 draw between the two teams at Charlton with a free-kick, and one of the goals in Arsenal's 2–1 home win over Charlton with a header from a cross, from the right, by Patrick Vieira. 'People like Henry are not looked upon as world-class strikers for nothing,' Day pointed out.

The same sentiments were expressed by Leeds United's manager Eddie Gray after Henry's best scoring performance of the season against the struggling Yorkshire club at Highbury in April 2004. In addition to operating with a conventional back four, Leeds, short of midfielders, also had two central defenders, Lucas Radebe and Dominic Matteo, in front of them. But Arsenal thrashed them 5–0, Henry scoring four of the goals, including a penalty. It was the first time an Arsenal player had scored that many in a game since Ian Wright against Everton fourteen years earlier. A number of observers felt that Leeds had made it easy for Henry by defending too 'high' up the field. But then, as their assistant manager Kevin Blackwell pointed out, Henry, with his ability to take on opponents and fire the ball into the net from long range, is quite happy against deeper defensive units as well. 'That pace is only part of the Henry package,' Blackwell said. 'OK, he is exceptionally quick, but this would not count for as much as it does if he was not such an intelligent player. He has a wonderful football brain, and that is possibly his greatest asset.'

Indeed, footballing intelligence is a key factor in how almost all the other successful scoring machines work.

CHAPTER TWO
MASTERS OF DECEPTION

'Strikers will always have the edge
because they are proactive
while the defenders are reactive.
Defenders have to work off
what the strikers do, not vice versa.'
ANDY ROXBURGH

The difference between Thierry Henry and many other strikers in the speeds with which their legs can carry them can be likened to that of a Ferrari and a Ford Escort. But, as Andy Roxburgh pointed out, 'Blistering pace is not the be all and end all. There are plenty who, while not particularly quick across the ground, have made up for it with their speed of thought.'

There can be no better illustration of this in modern-day football than Teddy Sheringham. As the vast majority of goals are scored from deep inside the penalty area, it should surprise nobody that Sheringham, physically one of the slowest of the top ten all-time Premiership scorers even when he was at his peak, is as high as fifth on the list. Sheringham has had the advantage of being able to score with headers as well as shots, of course. More important, however, is that although he has always struggled to go past opponents with the ball, he is a master at shielding it or laying it off, and then making the off-the-ball runs into the right positions for him to deliver the finishing touch.

His image as the 'thinking man's footballer' says it all, as indeed he did in an interview on the subject when he was with Manchester

United. Reminded of Terry Venables' view about the importance of a striker 'asking a defender questions', he said, 'You say to a centre-half, "If I go over here, what are you going to do about it?" or "If I go over there, what are you going to do about it?" Giggsy [Ryan Giggs] will be asking a different question: "Can you match me for pace?" If his defender can, he'll find another way because he's a clever footballer, and clever footballers find a way.

'I am sure there is a perception that I keep going so well because my game is not that taxing. Steve McClaren [then United's assistant manager] came to me a little while ago and he's got this new gimmick that tells how much a particular player runs in a game. He came to me and said, "You don't half do a lot of running." And I looked at him and said, "Don't tell me you've been sucked in by all the people who say I play an easy game?" I come off the pitch knackered after every game. Just because I don't sprint like a lot of players doesn't mean I'm standing still waiting for the ball to come.'

Whether it is outside the box or inside, the basic principles of his movement – the ability to elude markers – are the same. For all strikers, it is one of the key common denominators in the art of scoring, along with the desire to score: being able to anticipate where the ball is going and the willingness to take hard knocks, physically and psychologically.

It could be argued that the 'desire' to score applies to most outfield players, whatever their positions or roles. Even goalkeepers take delight in putting the ball in the net when given the opportunity to do so in training matches. However, for strikers, that desire is so strong that it can often be an obsession. Propelling the ball into the net – the very sight and sound of it hitting the back of the net – is like a drug to them. Some have pointed out that their need for that 'fix' is so powerful that they do not necessarily need to have beaten a goalkeeper or anybody else to get it. Ian Wright once said: 'Anybody who plays up front and says they're happy to see the team win even if they do not score is a liar. Sometimes you say that because you don't want a big-headed image, but deep in your heart, you know it is rubbish. I am desperate for goals, they are what my job is all about, and if I am not scoring – even if the team is winning – I sulk.'

At times like this, not all strikers are as difficult to live with as Wright was. Even so, when you talk to them about what scoring means to them you quickly appreciate that they care more deeply about it than most other players, and not just because scoring is their job. 'You are right, it is an obsession,' admitted Dion Dublin, the former Manchester United, Coventry and Aston Villa striker. He then mentioned a Villa match in which one of their players broke down the left wing, following a corner by the opposition, with Alan Thompson and himself charging down the middle in the hope of connecting with any cross. As the ball came over, Thompson was in a better position to put it into the net than Dublin was. 'But as far as I was concerned, it was my chance,' Dublin said. 'I had worked all week for that moment; I had run sixty or seventy yards to get on the end of that ball and nobody was going to stop me. As Alan was about to head it, I was literally screaming, "Dion's!" I was about ten yards away and I just launched myself at the ball. I caught it a peach, right in the top corner.'

John Aldridge was clearly not the type to give up a scoring chance either. 'I always wanted to be a top scorer,' he said. 'As a boy growing up in Liverpool my idol was Roger Hunt [the scorer of a record number of 245 goals for Liverpool], and I imagined myself as him when I used to practise for hours on a bit of wasteground alongside my home. You know, when I got a goal, it wasn't John Aldridge who had scored, it was Roger Hunt. For me, that love of scoring – the determination to score – was always there, although if anybody can take any credit for making it stronger it's Len Ashurst

[Newport County's manager at the start of Aldridge's professional career with the club]. I remember him saying to me, "You are scoring an average of one goal every three games at the moment, but if you want to be a top striker, it has to be one goal every two games." That advice always stuck in my mind. I spent all my career chasing that one-in-two ratio. During the spells that it dropped, even slightly, I would be panicking.'

Nobody can have loved scoring more than Aldridge, who got more goals in senior matches than any other player in the history of English football. In a career spanning nineteen years, from 1979 to 1998, he got 90 in 213 games for Newport, 90 in 141 for Oxford United, 63 in 104 for Liverpool, 40 in 75 for Real Sociedad, 174 in 287 for Tranmere and 19 in 69 for the Republic of Ireland. The grand total of 476 in 889 games put him nine ahead of Jimmy Greaves (who had the distinction of having scored all his goals in the top flight) and fourteen ahead of Arthur Rowley (who holds the British record for the highest number of league goals with his total of 434 in 619 matches for West Bromwich Albion, Fulham, Leicester and Shrewsbury between 1946 and 1965). The other particularly impressive individual scoring records in English football have been those of Dixie Dean, who scored 60 league goals in 39 First Division matches for Everton in the 1927/28 season and a total of 310 in 362 for the club at this level.

Greaves, because of his short, slight build and his brilliance on the ball in creating chances on his own, could be described as the odd man out in this group. Of the others, one similarity was that they all had outstanding anticipation inside the box. Another was that they all benefited from the service they received from the flanks. 'Losing my markers to get on the end of balls into the box from wide areas was always my forte,' Aldridge said. This was particularly important to him, and to Liverpool when they bought him from Oxford for £750,000 in January 1987. Liverpool, under the management of Kenny Dalglish, were preparing for the departure of Ian Rush to Juventus that summer and initially Aldridge, having never played in the First Division before, didn't strike many as the best choice as a partner for Rush, let alone a potential replacement for the Welshman. But Aldridge, more of an out-and-out finisher than Rush, pointed out, 'With Rush in the side, and especially when he had Kenny Dalglish alongside him up front, much of Liverpool's attacking play had been through the middle. Because of my ability to score from crosses, I was able to give them something extra.' The potential for him to do so was increased during the summer with the signings of Peter Beardsley, a player more comfortable in the build-up play than he was, and, most crucially, winger John Barnes. 'With Barnes on one flank and Ray Houghton [his Republic of Ireland and former Oxford team-mate] on the other, it was bingo for me.'

That had certainly been the case with Dixie Dean and Arthur Rowley. When they were giving goalkeepers sleepless nights the game was much more open and attack-orientated than it is today. Almost every team operated with wingers; indeed, the sight of such men attempting to get behind the opposing defence by taking on the opposing full-back – usually the only player they had to beat – and delivering the ball into the middle was an integral part of British football. Getting the ball into the box from wide positions is still recognised as an important aspect of goalscoring, but 'traditional' wing-play has become conspicuous by its absence. In the old days, the main aim of the wingers was to cross the ball from on or close to the goal-line so that the ball would be swinging away from defenders and into their forwards. Most defenders argue that such crosses, or pull-backs, are the most difficult for them to deal with. As for the men for whom the crosses are intended, Andy Roxburgh said, 'The

easiest balls for a player to hit or head are those that come into him.'
Little wonder that they were relished by Dean, a great header of the
ball, and Rowley, a wonderful striker of the ball with his left foot.

However, England's World Cup win in 1966, with a 4–4–2
system in which there was no place for conventional wingers,
marked a change in the styles of play of wide players throughout the
game. There was a greater onus on them to defend; indeed, wingers
as the likes of Dean and Rowley would have recognised them were
largely replaced by wingers-cum-midfielders. This, combined with
teams giving their full-backs more cover, led to a change in the
positions from which crosses were delivered. Instead of teams
getting the ball into the middle from on or close to the goal-line, they
were more liable to fire them in from deeper areas.

At one time, most wide men wanted to emulate Stanley
Matthews. Most recently, their role model has been David Beckham.
'He, more than anyone, has shown that you do not need to beat
people to get in good crosses,' Roxburgh said. 'In the old days, if you
received the ball on the wing, say twenty-five yards from goal, with a
defender in front of you, you would have been urging him to go and
dribble past him. But with people like Beckham, no. If they have a
defender in front of them, they are able to provide a great scoring
chance for a striker just by taking a slight touch to open up their
striking angle and bending the ball around their opponent.'

One advantage of an early cross – a cross delivered with the
minimum fuss and bother, without the wide player exploring his
dribbling potential or taking more touches on the ball than are
absolutely necessary – is that it makes it easier for a striker to 'read'
it. It might not create as much panic in a defence as one of those cut-
backs, but then given the right synchronisation between the player
making the cross and the striker for whom it is intended, this is of
little consequence. When an attack is developing down a flank, the

positioning of the striker can make it increasingly difficult (and ultimately impossible) for his marker to see both him and the ball at the same time. 'He has to take his eyes off you to check where the ball is at some time,' Roxburgh pointed out. 'It might only be for a split second, but that is enough for you to break free of him.' The most common striker ploy is for him to move on to his marker's blind side and make his run for the ball across him. So there's nothing more frustrating for a striker than for him to make a run off his marker in anticipation of the ball coming in only for a delay in the delivery to force him to stop, pull out and do it all again. 'It's even worse when the crosses keep going behind or over the bar,' Dion Dublin added. 'That really does do your head in.'

Even at the best of times, even in teams totally dominating the opposition, being a striker is harder work than many people might think. The art of scoring is often attributed to strikers just having the knack of being in the right place at the right time. Some of the goals they score – as a result of the most glaring and uncharacteristic of defensive errors, or scruffy strikes with parts of their anatomy other than their head or feet – even suggest that they have been born under a luckier star than other players. But though intuition and good fortune do come into it, this is largely because of the footballing intelligence and mentalities of the top scorers.

One of the major differences between defenders and strikers is the way they are 'programmed'. Defenders need to perform as though they are born pessimists, whereas strikers have to approach situations like eternal optimists. For strikers, that means always expecting (or anticipating) an incident that will give them a scoring chance. For example, when a goalkeeper makes a save without being able to hold the ball, how often do we see a striker reacting more quickly to the rebound than the defenders to stick it into the net? It also means strikers being prepared to continue making runs into scoring positions no matter how many times they have done so previously without receiving the ball.

Imagine what it must have been like for strikers to play against the superbly organised defence of Arsenal when the Gunners were managed by George Graham and had that famous back-line of Lee Dixon, Tony Adams, Steve Bould (or Martin Keown) and Nigel Winterburn pushing up to squeeze the play and working the offside trap to perfection. Their defence did even better under Arsene Wenger by establishing the record for conceding the fewest goals in a Premiership season: 17 in 38 matches in the 1998/99 season. But there were even fewer chances for strikers against the 1978/79 Liverpool defence, which still holds the record for the least number of goals conceded in a season in any division: just 16 in 42 matches, and two of them were own goals.

'You can be sure that all the men who scored against Liverpool were pleased to get into a hot bath afterwards,' said Graeme Sharp, the former Everton and Scotland centre-forward. 'Really, it's the same in a lot of matches. People do not fully appreciate the work you put in. When it comes to making runs into scoring positions you are always working on the law of averages. That [the unproductive run by a striker] is the unglamorous side of being a goalscorer. It can be soul-destroying when you make run after run after run without getting a scoring chance. It's easy to think, "This is not going to be my day." But you can guarantee that the moment you switch off, the one time that you don't make the run, that will be the time the ball will go in there. That is the thought that keeps you going.'

At the height of Sharp's career in the 1980s, in an Everton team that twice won the championship and also got their hands on the FA Cup and European Cup Winners' Cup, many of the goals that were to enable him to become the club's highest post-war scorer could be attributed to his understanding with Trevor Steven on the right flank and Kevin Sheedy on the left. 'I don't think any team before or since has shown a better understanding of the 4–4–2 system than Everton did,' he claimed. 'OK, people felt we were quite a basic team, but that was our strength. It suited me as much as it did anybody. Kevin's style of play was particularly good for me. I always knew that when he had the ball on his left foot around the halfway line, if I came towards the ball and spun off into the space between the centre-half and the full-back, he would find me with the ball and I would be one-on-one with the keeper. I look at the way my goal record declined when I played with wide men such as Peter Beagrie and Pat Nevin. They were wonderful players, don't get me wrong, but there were times when, before crossing the ball, they would want to take that extra touch or two.'

Brighton manager Mark McGhee, the former Morton, Newcastle United, Aberdeen, Hamburg and Celtic striker, recalled a similar situation. 'I went from one team who gave me the ball early [Aberdeen] to one who didn't [Hamburg]. At Aberdeen, Alex Ferguson had created a team that was good for strikers. You can make the best runs in the world, but if you don't have players who can give you the right ball at the right time then they are meaningless. We had Gordon Strachan for a start; the vast majority of my goals, indeed the majority of the team's goals, came from his passes or crosses. It's a standing joke between us that, though I thought I was making good runs, all I was doing was chasing his passes. Apart from Gordon on the right flank, we had the added bonus of Peter Weir [a conventional winger] on the left. That gave us the sort of penetration down the flanks that the great Celtic team of the 1960s had. My clearest memories of that Celtic team are of midfielders like Bobby Murdoch and Bobby Auld hitting balls with backspin right into the corners for Tommy Gemmell and Jim Craig [the attacking full-backs], and the balls being cut back hard and low from the goal-line. That is what Gordon and Peter could do. I once scored a hat-trick in a European game and all the goals were identical: balls being fired across from the goal-line, with people like me piling in to attack them with runs across the defenders.

'Aberdeen were a high-tempo team, and the idea of me joining Hamburg was sold to me partly on the basis of their being a high-tempo side as well. Well, they had been at one time, but with ageing stars such as Felix Magath they had become much more of a possession-driven team. I would work the whole line [the full width of the field] at Aberdeen – I was the type who ran the opposition into the ground – but I quickly realised it was pointless in a number of my Hamburg matches because the pace of the game was slower. Everything was being played through Magath and he was unwilling to really take any chances on possession being lost. When I did get the ball, it was usually to my feet, but because of the earlier runs I had made without getting the ball it wasn't the opposition who were liable to be knackered, it was me. Because of the delays in the ball coming to me, there were some games in which I was standing still.

'You can do that in some areas, of course. One guy who always used to fascinate me was Ruud Gullit [the former AC Milan and Holland forward]. He used to find space without moving. When the ball is on the flanks, it's natural for defenders to want to move back to protect their goal. So, if Gullit positioned himself on the edge of the penalty area, he would get the ball while standing still. He was clever – he knew what he was doing. But in most other attacking situations you have to work for your openings.'

Indeed, all the goalscoring experts I spoke to insisted that it is essential for strikers to be on the move all the time, especially in the box. Their message was: 'Movement creates space.' Once you are standing still, you are finished.

Among the British strikers noted for their intelligent movement was Gordon Wallace, the former Dundee player who is second only to Ally McCoist on the top post-war scorers list in Scotland. Wallace said, 'I think all leading scorers are born with an instinct for scoring, but you can add to it. Not being the quickest of strikers, I was taught about movement in the box at the very start of my career, and I worked very hard at it. When we are talking about the movement to lose your marker and get to the ball for a strike at goal, you are often only talking about gaining half a yard, if that.'

Most of that movement is based on the principle of strikers taking markers away from the areas they wish to go into – running away from the ball rather than towards it. Sometimes it might only involve a few steps: one or two in one direction, followed by a spurt in another. That is what strikers mean when they talk about 'one run for him, one for me'. Other basic movement guidelines for strikers in their battle of wits with defenders are 'run long to go short and short to go long' (when using the length of the field) and 'run in to go out, out to go in' (when using the width of the field). On top of this are the fundamental rules relating to the geometry of forward passes and forward runs: 'Straight pass, diagonal run – diagonal pass, straight run.'

It is difficult to imagine any striker having covered more ground in his attempts to elude his markers and create the right finishing angles than Alan Shearer did when he was at his physical peak. At one time, his runs to get the better of defenders would be made anywhere in the last third of the field. If an attack was developing down the right, it wasn't unusual for Shearer to start his quest to eventually get on the end of the ball by taking his marker virtually across to the other side. At times he seemed to take the principle of strikers making their first scoring runs away from the ball to the extreme.

Kevin Keegan, the Newcastle manager who signed him for the club and who had also appeared to have an inexhaustible supply of running power when he was a striker, was all for it. Less enthusiastic about it was Keegan's successor, Ruud Gullit. It is no secret that Shearer's relationship with the Dutchman was not as harmonious as it had been with his previous managers. Indeed, this was well and truly brought into the open in March 2004 when Gullit, in a News of the World interview, accused Shearer of being a 'rotten apple'. 'He thinks about himself all the time,' the Dutchman said. 'It is always about his goals and not about the team. I knew I had to change it if we were to succeed. I needed to change the way Alan Shearer played, but he did not want to change. In fact, he made it plain he did not want to play for me.' According to Gullit, his disagreements with Shearer stemmed partly from his view that the striker spent too much time outside the box. 'As the manager, I wanted him to play well and to score goals. But I wanted to use him in a different way. I asked him to move into the penalty box more, rather than keep running wide to the left and wide to the right and leaving the area empty. That's all. But after a while, he made it clear he did not want to.' Shearer declined to make any public comment on this, although to those who would argue that many of his goals came because of the distances he ran to get the better of his markers, not in spite of them, he didn't need to.

Today, at the tail-end of his career, it's a different story. As one would expect of a striker in his mid-thirties, with his list of war wounds, Shearer has had to change. In the 2003/04 season, with Newcastle possessing other attacking players to do the long-distance runs, Shearer's own runs were restricted to shorter and more central bursts inside the box. 'I think I spend a lot more time with my back to the goal [receiving the ball in central areas] than I did at Southampton and Blackburn,' he said. However, thanks to his grasp of those basic movement principles, not to mention his combativeness and determination, he still ended the campaign second only to Thierry Henry in the Premiership scoring list.

Of course, defenders are not unaware of the ways in which Shearer and other leading strikers create their shooting or heading space. But, as Roxburgh pointed out, 'The strikers will always have the edge because they are proactive while the defenders are reactive. Defenders have to work off what the strikers do, not vice versa. Having said that, a lot can depend on how it [the decoy movement] is carried out, and the timing of it. Alex Ferguson has said that this is probably the hardest thing to coach. I agree. You can teach people how to lose a man – the theory – but being able to time the run well enough to avoid getting into a potential scoring position too early or too late is another matter. The timing of the run into the scoring position is probably even more important than the finish itself. A shot can still go in even if you miss-hit it. Quite honestly, miss-hitting can sometimes be the best move. But if your movement is not timed properly, you are lost. Some people claim that it's down to natural instinct. There's no doubt that some people do have a natural instinct for it, but I would suggest that it also boils down to footballing intelligence, and the ability to read the game. You have to be able to anticipate things. The top strikers are so good at it that when they get the ball in the box they seem to have twice as much time as anybody else.'

No contest of football intelligence between a defender and striker can have been more absorbing than the one that the great Liverpool centre-back, Alan Hansen, conducted with Karl-Heinz Rummenigge in the 1981 European Cup semi-finals. 'He presented me with probably my biggest ever European Cup challenge,' Hansen recalled. 'He was brillliant at making diagonal runs for the ball, across me, and for a while, only my speed enabled me to stop him getting away from me. But I knew I was living on borrowed time and it was only about 20 minutes into the second leg that I was able to come up with a better solution. As the ball was about to be played through to him, I just took a step or two into the space into which he wanted to move, which put him off. But he did eventually score, so although Liverpool won, I cannot say that I overcame the challenge with flying colours.'

That there is a lot more to scoring, and especially the build-up to it, than often meets the eye quickly becomes apparent when you discuss the subject with Mark McGhee. 'A lot of strikers are instinctive players,' McGhee said. 'You can see that when they are called upon to make an instinctive finish they have no problems executing that, but when they are given a lot of time, that can be a problem to them. But they also tend to be intelligent players. I played very much off the cuff when I first started playing league football at Morton, but the more I progressed, the more I was forced to think about what I was doing. At Morton, I just ran around; my game was totally unstructured. It was the same when I stepped up into the old First Division with Newcastle, which is what worked against me there. I was playing against guys like Gordon McQueen [Leeds] and Billy Bonds [West Ham], and because of their positional sense, their footballing intelligence, they could more or less just step back and watch me. I was virtually running into them.

'The turning point for me came when I joined Aberdeen, and worked with Alex Ferguson. Up to then, though I had scored goals and created chances for others, nobody had really talked to me about the other aspects of the role – the sort of little foundation stones. I wasn't really sure what my starting points in a game were. Alex gave me lots of little targets. For example, one of the first things he said to me was, "You have to make sure that you win the first ball." That was my starting point. Then he said to me, "OK, you won the first ball, but you lost the next two." From then on I knew that I had to compete for every ball; that if a move broke down and the ball was played to the opposing full-back I had to try and stop him settling on it; and so on. So suddenly I had a list of challenges or objectives which gave me a focus I'd never had before.

'As with players in other positions, you are learning and developing all the time. Apart from Alex, I also picked up a lot at Aberdeen from Steve Archibald [his striking partner]. He was brilliant at anticipating where the ball was going to go, and in that way he was probably the striker who had the biggest influence on me.'

Coincidentally, at the time of my interview with McGhee during the 2003/04 season, when he was Millwall manager, he had been studying the movement of the club's centre-forward, Neil Harris. The player, signed from the non-league club Cambridge City in March 1998 for a fee of £30,000, had quickly become one of the most respected strikers outside the Premiership. In the 1999/2000 campaign he became the first Millwall player to score 25 goals in a season since Teddy Sheringham in 1990/91, and the following season his 28 goals helped steer Millwall to promotion from the Second Division. But then he was diagnosed with testicular cancer, which put him out of action for the first half of the season.

Not surprisingly, it took time for Harris to regain his old sharpness and to adjust to the higher demands of the First Division, and he was going through a barren scoring spell when I met McGhee. 'I think he is not scoring at the moment simply because he is running out of the right positions as opposed to running into them,' McGhee explained. 'He is a very willing player, he loves to make runs, but we have just been talking to him about narrowing them, keeping himself more in the eighteen-yard box. At the moment he's making runs into the corners, and in trying to hold the ball up or beat people there not really giving himself much of a chance to get himself back in the box. A lot of it is to do with confidence. He's not the quickest of players, and in the First Division, where defenders are quicker than those in the Second, maybe he feels that he needs to put himself in areas where he is going to get a bit more time and space. I think that happens a lot with strikers who are not particularly quick. But those are not the areas in which they are going to score goals. I know that my best performances as a striker came in matches where I kept myself in the eighteen-yard box. Apart from anything else, if you are on the ball in there, defenders are always wary of committing themselves. For Neil, and other promising strikers, these sorts of things are just part of the learning process.'

By the end of the 2003/04 season, Harris's scoring record was still not as impressive as it had been in the Second Division. But, as with all strikers in teams with high-scoring midfielders, his movement in creating space for others did help Tim Cahill and Paul Ifill make up for it. Harris, indeed, was a regular member of the Millwall team that under the management of Dennis Wise reached the FA Cup final for the first time in their history.

Teddy Sheringham is among the most obvious strikers for any aspiring scorer on a learning curve to study, but when it comes to the 'tricks' of their trade, they would all benefit from some tuition from Graeme Sharp as well. Many of his opponents in the 1980s will readily confirm that he was the striker they least relished facing; and among those at the top of the Sharp Appreciation Society list is Alan Hansen. He once recalled that he was always 'twitchy' when up against opponents who attempted to turn their confrontations with him into contests of strength and aggression.

The most physically intimidating striker he faced was Billy Whitehurst, a journeyman number 9 who nonetheless was so powerful and combative that Hansen admitted he was almost scared of him. 'But,' he added, 'I would get even twitchier if the striker also had as much footballing intelligence as Graeme Sharp. He was probably the British striker for whom I had the greatest respect. If anybody had a perfect grasp of all the aspects of centre-forward play, all the little tricks of the trade, it was him. Graeme was not the type who could dribble past three or four defenders, but in all the less noticeable aspects of centre-forward play he was a master. He was a physical player who developed into an excellent technical player, a terrific all-round striker, because of his intelligence. He played in my area when I was Liverpool's left-side central defender; it was the ideal position for him because of his ability as the target for those sweeping diagonal passes from Kevin Sheedy. His movement to attack the ball was superb. The whole defence had to be on its toes when he was around. The one thing you could be sure about was that the experience of playing against him would leave you mentally drained.'

It could also leave you with some physical aches and pains as well. One of the less desirable aspects of scoring concerns the importance of strikers being prepared to go into areas where they are bound to suffer painful physical knocks – 'areas where it hurts', as they put it. Thanks to the stricter interpretation of the laws by referees, defenders can no longer dish out as much physical punishment to strikers as they once did. Even so, the conflict between the two sets of players close to goal – full of tugs, digs and pushes at the very least – quickly separates the men from the boys.

The very mention of this in Frank McLintock's sitting room was enough to cause him to become animated enough to rise from his chair to give a demonstration. 'I cannot believe it when I see some of today's central defenders,' he said. 'When the ball is on the wing, some of them – even Rio Ferdinand – can be looking for the ball [instead of the man they are marking] for five or six seconds. I know you cannot ignore the ball, but when I was a central defender I used to keep touching the striker. It would be touch-look, touch-look, touch-look. If I could not feel him I would back into him, and if he tried to connect with the ball I would block him.' At this point, McLintock showed how to stop a striker attacking the ball with a run across him by sweeping his arm into his opponent's stomach. 'As soon as he started his run, I would bloody whack him. It knocks him back a little bit – you can sometimes actually hear him catching his breath – and it also has the effect of propelling you forward. You don't mess around either when you're going for the ball in the air. You might know that you are not going to win the ball, but the main thing is that you throw yourself at the ball so that the other guy cannot get a clean contact.'

All of which makes you realise what strikers are getting at when they talk about the need not to allow themselves to be 'pushed around', and why professionals have rated Sharp so highly. 'When it came to gaining an advantage over defenders, he seemed to know everything there was to know,' said Hansen. 'One feature of his game was that when the ball was in the air he made it difficult for the defender marking him to get the ball without fouling him.' Sharp, who now employed at Everton as the club's fan liaison officer, and hosts a local radio football phone-in programme, acknowledged, 'I won a lot of free-kicks in those situations. If our team were playing a ball from the back to the front, I had a habit of jumping early and backwards. It was just one of a number of little things that you knew you could get away with.'

On the subject of strikers being able to 'look after themselves', Sharp said, 'My brother, Richard, who played a couple of games as a striker for Rangers but failed to establish himself in the top flight, was probably a better footballer than me. But he did not go further because he wasn't hard enough. My father always used to say, "Don't let anyone make a mug of you." That was his advice to me when I came to Everton as a raw teenager, because if somebody kicked me I was inclined to go into my shell a little bit. One of my first matches was against Leeds United, when they had Kenny Burns playing for them. It shows how naive I was then because I was thinking, "Oh, a fellow Scot, a Scottish international, he should be OK with you." When we got on the field the first thing he said was, "I am going to break your leg." I thought, "Oh-oh." My father's words were ringing in my ears.

'I learnt a lot from Bobby Latchford [Everton's first-choice centre-forward when Sharp arrived at Goodison]. Whenever I think of Bob, I think about the time I first played with him in a pre-season competition in Spain. I had heard so much about him, about his not allowing defenders to take liberties with him, and I could not understand it because he was getting kicked from pillar to post in that game. I thought, "What is going on here?" But then, all of a sudden, Bob literally made his mark on the centre-half – he had to be carried off – and scored at the same time. I could not work out how he'd done it. It intrigued me.

'Then Bob left and Andy Gray came in, and I would say I learnt more about the so-called tricks of the trade from Andy than I did from anybody else. He was the one who really encouraged me to be more aggressive and not to get pushed around so much. I was never a dirty player, but if it was necessary for me to stand up for myself in that way, then so be it. Some people [defenders] will do anything to put you off and you have to be prepared to deal with it. Only the other day I had an argument with this caller on my radio show who was having a go at Alan Shearer for the way he got stuck into defenders. "He is an animal," he said. I said, "Hold on a minute. If he is up there getting kicked all over the place he has to look after himself."'

Dion Dublin nodded in agreement. 'I like the physical side of the game, getting stuck in, and the verbal side. It's a man's game, and it's all about how mentally strong you are to take all the abuse. I find it very stimulating. It's good, it's good.'

The need for mental toughness, of course, also applies to that moment when a striker, having eluded his marker to get into a scoring position, is ready to apply the finishing touch. Quite often it looks as if he should be able to score with his eyes closed, but that's assuming he hasn't thought about what the repercussions might be if he misses.

CHAPTER THREE
TARGET PRACTICE

'I hate it when some of the lads I work
with put a shot wide, and then laugh
over it. They think it's funny,
but it really does my head in.'

BRYAN 'POP' ROBSON

TARGET PRACTICE

When Malcolm Christie had a run with Derby County of fifteen matches without a goal towards the end of the 2000/01 season, the young striker was encouraged to discuss his problems with the club's sports psychologist, Bill Beswick. After Christie and other members of the coaching staff had gone through the various physical and technical aspects of his play, Beswick posed what proved to be the key question. Referring to a chance Christie had missed in the last game, he asked, 'What were you thinking about at the moment you hit the ball?'

'The boss [manager Jim Smith],' Christie replied. 'As I was about to shoot, I thought about him looking at me and saying, "For Christ's sake, Malcolm, how did you miss that?"'

So the answer was simple: Christie was clearly allowing negative thoughts to enter his mind; or, as Beswick put it, he was suffering from 'emotional static' (the 'scientific expression', he told me). As Christie's problems were all in his mind it was only to be expected that Beswick should take the lead role in helping him get rid of them. The result of this was that in the shooting practice that was organised for him, Christie had to shout a word at every moment of impact –

an action which, Beswick explained, was designed to immediately clear his mind of all thoughts outside that of hitting the ball well enough to put it in the net. 'We refer to it as the "break" or "trigger" word,' Beswick said. 'When we tried it with Ashley Ward [another Derby County striker] he preferred to use the word "net", because he told us that he loved to see the net bulge, whereas Malcolm chose "ball". The shooting practice we gave him became increasingly more difficult, and as a further test of his ability to concentrate we even ended up screaming and shouting at him to try and put him off.'

This work was followed by Derby's penultimate match of the season, against Manchester United at Old Trafford. United had already clinched the Premiership title but the view that Derby could capitalise on any mood of relaxation in the United camp was offset by the fact that the visitors were as low as seventeenth in the table, just one place above the relegation zone, and had achieved only one previous away win. But Derby beat United 1–0, and Christie, after an excellent run followed by the shout 'Ball!' and an explosive left-foot shot, scored the goal of his life. Beswick recalled, 'Shortly after the game, I asked him how it felt. "Great," he said. I then asked what was in his mind when he was about to strike the ball, and he couldn't tell me. He had concentrated so much on the finish that he could not even tell me anything about the build-up to the goal. This is common among top-class strikers. It [scoring] becomes so instinctive to them that they just cannot explain how they have done it. All Malcolm could remember was that he hit the ball with his left foot. That was it.' The following week, Christie scored another goal that brought Derby a 1–1 draw against fifth-place Ipswich Town.

Beswick, a former basketball coach whose expertise in the mind-over-matter field has also been put to use for the England youth and under-21 squads, is one of a number of sports psychologists (or 'mental coaches' as some like to call themselves) to have become involved in professional football in Britain in recent years. Two other well-known members of the breed are John Syer, who has been linked with Tottenham at various times over a period spanning some 25 years, and Willi Raillo, the Norwegian who helps Sven-Goran Eriksson get his England players in the right frame of mind. But they have not gone as far in the game as Beswick.

In addition to Jim Smith, another colleague at Derby who thought highly of him was Steve McClaren, then the first-team coach. So much so that McClaren, on joining Manchester United as Sir Alex Ferguson's right-hand man, persuaded his boss to sign up Beswick in a consultancy capacity. Then, when McClaren became Middlesbrough manager, he brought Beswick with him, and even appointed him assistant manager. The only other sports psychologist to have filled that sort of position at a leading professional football club in England has been the Frenchman Jacques Crevoisier. At the time of Beswick's Middlesbrough appointment, Gérard Houllier brought Crevoisier to Liverpool as his first-team coach.

The language such men use, which can come across as the application of psycho-babble to the obvious, can be irritating to the more dyed-in-the-wool members of the professional football fraternity. Also, in the macho environment of a soccer dressing room, nobody likes to think of himself as a suitable case for treatment. As one sports psychologist has remarked, 'One of the problems of dealing with some professional footballers and managers is that they confuse psychology with psychiatry.' Recalling his first few months working at Derby, Beswick said, 'The players recoiled in horror at the idea of working with a "shrink". Even Jim Smith expected some guy in a white coat.'

However, the credibility barrier they have faced has become smaller. Indeed, because of the ever-growing pressure on managers and teams to achieve success, men like Beswick could be described as essential to them rather than helpful, not least in their dealings with strikers. 'These are very vulnerable people,' Beswick pointed out. 'It is often said that a striker is never going to take all of his chances – he might only take one in six or eight – and therefore he has to be prepared to fail. He needs to have the courage to miss in order to have the courage to score. In my basketball days, I remember a prolific shooter being asked where his confidence came from, and him replying, "I decided early in my career to shoot it up and live in the streets." What he meant was that he was going to shoot at every opportunity, and if they went in, fine, he would be a hero, and if they didn't, he was quite prepared to pay the price for it. I often apply that quote to goalscorers.

'That is not to say that they are all the same. A lot of them do live a life of great peaks and troughs. They are either in sunshine or rain. But you can learn to cope with it, and I think the great strikers are able to use it to their advantage They thrive on anxiety, to the point where they actually invite it.' In that sense, Beswick agreed that the top scorers are a bit like journalists who tend to be at their best when writing to tight deadlines, 'when the pressure is really on'. He said that, in his experience, the trait of creating extra pressure and using it to one's advantage is common to many leading sportsmen and sportswomen.

As an example of another form of this, he recalled the approach of the great American sprinter Michael Johnson to the 1996 Olympic Games in Atlanta. 'In the build-up, Johnson announced to the press that he was not just going to achieve the 200- and 400-metre gold medal double [which had never been done before], but that he was also going to break the world 200 metres record. It might have seemed perverse for him to put that added pressure on himself, but in an event in which he was such a hot favourite he felt he needed it to be able to properly motivate himself.' Johnson was as good as his word, but then the work he had put into his bid for Olympic glory in training, allied to his natural talent, did much to help make this an inevitability.

In soccer, all scorers recognise the importance of regular practice of their kicking techniques. As many are keen golfers, they are inclined to liken the shooting repetition work they do to that of the top tournament professionals in striving to improve their swings and their putting. This can be misleading; whether all Premiership and Nationwide League scorers put in as many training-ground hours on their finishing as they could and should do is a moot point. As John Aldridge recalled, the 'laziness' of some of his strikers when he was Tranmere Rovers' manager 'drove me mad'. As a striker himself, Aldridge said he thought nothing of staying on the training ground after completing his work with the team to improve the aspects of the game particularly relevant to himself. 'I loved practising my shooting. When I was away with the Irish Republic squad, I did so much of it before games that Jack Charlton [the manager] would sometimes have to come and virtually drag me off the field. But it was different with some of the strikers I was associated with at Tranmere. Once the team training sessions had finished they just wanted to get in their cars and go home as quickly as possible.'

Some strikers do have a reasonable excuse for this. Southampton's James Beattie, referring to the high number of matches played by the leading teams in England (and possibly the amount of energy he expends during games), pointed out that strikers have to balance the requirement to hone their shooting skills against the need for them to get the right degree of rest, and to give their bodies some form of protection from unnecessary muscle strains.

However, it's not unusual for strikers to attribute an improvement in their scoring records to more shooting practice.

Certainly, in terms of that 'practice makes perfect' maxim they will have readily appreciated what the South African golfing legend Gary Player was getting at when he said, 'The more I practise, the luckier I get.'

The example set in England's rugby union squad by Jonny Wilkinson and his kicking coach Dave Alred will have been of more than merely passing interest to them as well. To say that the pair's approach to the art of scoring points from penalties and drop goals has been an obsession is putting it mildly. In their quest for perfection in mind and body, it would be virtually impossible to find any stone that they have left unturned.

In an intriguing article on Wilkinson in *The Guardian*, Richard Williams wrote, 'Together, Wilkinson and Alred practise for several hours a day, Alred standing behind the goal posts while Wilkinson kicks from every conceivable angle and range, going through his complex – and, to opponents, interminably protracted – routine before each attempt. Wilkinson finishes a session with a series of six kicks, but they all have to be perfect. If one of them misses, he starts again. He will not leave the pitch until he has sent six in a row whistling between the posts. That means stretching a session from two to three hours and sometimes beyond.' Part of that pre-kick routine, Williams pointed out, involved Wilkinson 'lowering his body into the posture of a man sitting on an invisible shooting-stick, and putting his hands together for several long seconds'. Williams continued, 'He told me that the hands are like a barrier erected against the outside world, helping him to cut out the tens of thousands of opposing fans who are likely to set up a barrage of whistles and jeers in an attempt to disturb his intense concentration.' He added, 'He [Wilkinson] imagines a jeering mouth behind the goal and attempts to send the ball down its throat. Another [psychological ploy] involves an imaginary woman called Doris who sits in a particular seat in the stand behind the goal, holding a can of Coke. As Wilkinson prepares to kick, he visualises the flight of the ball ending up in Doris's lap, knocking the drink out of her hands.'

In an interview with Jamie Jackson for the *Observer Sports Magazine*, Wilkinson gave a further insight into how deeply he and Alred think about this role. He talked about his concentration on the most important technical aspects of his kick – 'I know that if I get those one or two things right, the rest will take care of itself' – the numerous little mental 'keys' he uses to help make his kicking action 'aggressive and deliberate', and his visualisation techniques concerning where the ball is going to go. He added, 'You've done it thousands of times on the training ground, and that's what gives you your confidence.'

This will have been music to the ears of Beswick. Donning his soccer striker's hat, he remarked, 'There is an element about the job [of scoring] that is instinctive, and some are more instinctive than others. You look at people such as Thierry Henry. When they are shooting, they can think of nothing else but the action of scoring; other thoughts such as the goalkeeper, the crowd, the tackles about to hit them are blocked out. The top scorers are the ones who get into that state the most often. But, through practice, you can train yourself to do it. The more you practise it, the more your body will take over from the brain and the more successful you will be.'

For Beswick, this is precisely why players should practise penalties. Some managers argue that it is a futile exercise on the grounds that taking spot-kicks in training cannot compare with doing so under far greater pressure in a match situation. That, it will be recalled, was the stance Glenn Hoddle adopted when he was criticised for not making penalty practice an integral part of his team's preparations before the 1998 World Cup quarter-final against Argentina (when England were beaten in a penalty shoot-out).

However, Beswick's logic is difficult to dispute, not least among the men for whom the task of putting the ball in the net (by any means) is what they are being paid to do.

Ray Clarke, one of the few British strikers to have made a big impact on the Continent, certainly sees the sense in it. Now Southampton's chief scout, Clarke looked every inch a natural scorer as a boy, but he stresses that the ability which prompted Tottenham to sign him from school was also the product of hard work. 'I could always score a lot of goals in schoolboy football, but when I was twelve or thirteen my father bought me a basic skills coaching book called *Skilful Soccer*, and it became our soccer bible. He would spend hours helping me practise the various shooting and heading tips in it in our garage and the local park. I was a right-footed player, but by the time I came to Tottenham's attention I could hit the ball equally well with the left. People just could not work out what was my natural striking foot.'

Such was his ability as a teenager that Tottenham brought him into their first-team squad when he was just sixteen. 'I came very close to putting you in the team at that age,' the manager, Bill Nicholson, once told him. However, he was never able to make further progress. This was due partly to his inability at that time to handle Nicholson's demanding, brusque nature. 'I took what he said to me as criticism rather than guidance. I became very apprehensive about my ability.' Also, Clarke suggests that his inclusion in the first-team squad might have come too early. 'I don't think I worked as hard on my game as I should have done,' he admitted.

At 21, Clarke, after just one substitute appearance for Spurs, began a downward Football League journey, first to Second Division Swindon Town where he scored two goals in fourteen matches, and then to Fourth Division Mansfield Town where he was their top scorer in his first season with 28 goals in 46 league games, thus helping them gain promotion, and again the following season with 24 in 45. All this made a rejuvenated Clarke think that he could hack it at a higher grade, but even he was taken by surprise by the fact that the best opportunity to do so was offered by Sparta Rotterdam in the Dutch First Division. He was virtually unknown in Holland, and Sparta, who paid Mansfield £90,000 for him (a record fee for the English club), had never seen him play. According to Clarke, Sparta, searching for an English striker who could give them greater physical presence up front, took a chance on him on the recommendation of Bill McGarry, who had been manager of Wolves and had rejected the opportunity to take over at the Dutch club in favour of going to work in Saudi Arabia. All things being equal, Clarke would have preferred to join one of the English First Division clubs interested in him, but Sparta, apart from the transfer fee they were willing to pay, offered him a salary of £24,000 – more than six times what he had been getting at Mansfield.

However, as Clarke struggled to adjust to his new team, Sparta must have been cursing McGarry; despite the money he was raking in, Clarke might have been tempted to do so as well. He couldn't speak the language and he felt so much an outsider that he says he developed a siege mentality. 'I knew the players were talking about me behind my back,' he said. 'I caught one of them one day. We were in the dressing room, and the player glanced at me while making a remark in Dutch to another lad. The other lad could speak English, and when I asked what had been said he told me, "It is about time you scored some goals."' Not long afterwards Clarke ran into a member of the supporters' committee who had helped the club stump up the money for his transfer fee. 'We should send you back,' Clarke was told. 'You are no good.' Clarke added, 'The other players would wind me up about the comparatively low technical level of the game in England. It was them and me.'

It would probably have remained that way had Clarke not been forced to work harder on his finishing in training. The initiative for this came from Sparta's coach, Cor Brom, a former Ajax player whose quest to help Clarke justify Sparta's decision to sign him virtually turned into a personal crusade. 'There were only about five full-time pros at Sparta then and we trained in the afternoons,' Clarke recalled. 'But when Brom and I discussed the problems I was having, he said, "Right, as from now, you also come in every Tuesday and Thursday morning to do some training with me." Basically, for each of those mornings he set me a ninety-minute shooting and heading programme. It was all repetition work, and it was unbelievably intense. Everything was worked out in blocks of twenty, with Brom and the assistant coach standing either side of me with ten balls each, feeding them to me in quick succession. I went through every type of shot and header you can think of, from all manner of different angles, and the name of the game for me was that I had to hit the target. I don't know exactly how many shots and headers I had in each of those sessions – it must have been around three hundred – but the results were remarkable. After a while my failure rate was only about ten per cent, and as this started to be mirrored in my performances on a Saturday, it [practising scoring] became a bit like a drug. I started going in for extra finishing work even on my days off. I was happy just to get a bag of twenty balls and practise hitting them into an empty net on my own. I had started to achieve success and I had this burning urge to make sure it was maintained. I'd sometimes go in while taking my missus out shopping. I'd stop the car outside the ground and she would say, "I thought we were going shopping," and I'd say, "We are, but I need to do a bit [of shooting practice] first."'

Little wonder that Clarke became Sparta's highest scorer for fifteen years. His record in his two years there was 42 goals in 71 matches. Then came the ultimate step-up in the context of Dutch football: Brom was appointed Ajax's coach and he took Clarke with him. 'I went from being a big fish in a small pond to a small fish in a big pond,' said Clarke. Through his desire to retain that commitment to practice, though, the fish – the only non-international at Ajax – got a lot bigger. He achieved an even better scoring record at Ajax with 38 goals in 44 games. 'Being in a team of that calibre does make a big difference to a striker,' he acknowledged, 'but you still have to have the ability to stick the chances away.'

Increasingly troubled by a hip problem, Clarke did not have the same success at his next ports of call: Bruges in Belgium, Brighton and Hove Albion, and finally Newcastle. However, looking back on his work behind the scenes, he is grateful for having 'seen the light' when he did. 'If I was a club manager, I would make sure that my strikers did the same as I did. I cannot possibly see how practising a particular skill would not make someone better at it.'

In most shooting practice sessions, getting into the habit of just 'hitting the target', irrespective of whether the ball goes into the net, is the most rudimentary starting point. Bryan 'Pop' Robson, the coach of Leeds United's under-18 players, said, 'It doesn't matter if there isn't a goalkeeper there; the main thing is to get into the habit of getting that ball on target.' To Robson, this is not something to be taken lightly. 'I hate it when some of the lads I work with put a shot wide, and then laugh over it. They think it's funny, but it really does my head in.'

Robson, once described by Malcolm Macdonald as one of the best strikers of the ball he had seen, is one of a seemingly endless list of experts who look upon Jimmy Greaves as the ultimate shooting role model. Greaves's most famous characteristic as a finisher was his ability almost to pass the ball into the net. That, in fact, is a hallmark of all the truly great goalscorers. Ray Clarke, recalling his experience of training with Johann Cruyff for two months at Ajax when the Dutch master returned to the club to get himself fit for his testimonial match, said, 'He taught me that you don't have to lash the ball. Sometimes you get so fired up or anxious over a scoring chance you feel you have to hit the ball as hard as you can. "Great scorers just pass it," Cruyff told me. "Just relax."' In the modern game, another striker noted for not trying to burst the ball is Arsenal's Thierry Henry. Unless it is absolutely necessary for him to do otherwise, the Frenchman's shooting emphasis is very much on accuracy rather than power.

Still, in all my conversations on this shooting-pass subject with leading English football figures, Greaves was mentioned the most. Mervyn Day, a former goalkeeper, said, 'I played against Greaves in practice matches [when the pair were at West Ham] and what struck me about the goals he scored against me was that there was no power at all in a lot of his shots. It proved to me that there were quite a few situations in which a striker only needs to pass the ball accurately to beat the keeper. For example, imagine a situation where the striker has the ball just inside the penalty area. If the keeper is six or seven yards off his line, which he usually should be, that means you are only talking about a shot over eleven or twelve yards. Why blast the ball? This was why you hardly ever saw Greaves miss the target. You think about it.'

All the technical and psychological factors involved in the art of clinical finishing, especially with a pass-shot, are perhaps best epitomised in those agonising one-against-one situations when the striker is bearing down on the goal with only the keeper to beat, or is taking a penalty. Such moments, the ultimate cases of the so-called 'battle of wits' between strikers and keepers, can easily remind one of that gunfight showdown involving Gary Cooper and his arch enemy in High Noon. In the footballing equivalent, the striker and the keeper, in trying to force each other to make the first move, can often find the time they have to think about their actions considerably more of a handicap than an advantage. As virtually all of the pressure is on the striker, these situations have tended to produce the most embarrassing misses.

As far as penalties are concerned, Trevor Francis remarked, 'If they were as easy as they seemed, people would be fighting over taking them, which is not the case. However, it does surprise me when forwards don't put themselves forward for the job; I think it tells you something about what they are like mentally. You would think that if there is a chance of scoring, they more than anyone should grasp it. But some strikers don't want to because the price they have to pay for missing is too high for them. I think you will find that these are the strikers who allow not scoring to get to them the most.'

But if anything, one-on-ones in open play can be even more nerve-racking, given the number of ways in which a keeper can 'out-psyche' his opponent. Ray Clarke recalled that at Ajax, the advice he was given on how to be successful in such situations made him think he was being taken into the realm of unarmed combat. A member of the coaching staff kept telling him, 'Show no mercy [to keepers].' On the eve of some away matches, Clarke would find a picture of the opposing keeper pinned above his hotel bed with the message, 'Tomorrow, you kill him.'

Maybe it would have helped him more to have had some advice from someone such as Mervyn Day. Most keepers agree that it's important for them to stay on their feet for as long as possible, and that when a striker is coming towards them with the ball they are vulnerable to shots hit early, preferably with little backlift, as they are coming out to narrow the angle. 'Generally,' Day added, 'if you are one on one and are not going to try and take the ball around the keeper, there is a point when the best shot is the one close to a keeper's feet. Then there's the one through his legs. The closer you get to a keeper, the more he will crouch to cover the goal and the wider his feet will become.' Frank McLintock said, 'The keeper will come out ten to fifteen yards when a striker is running through, but sometimes I think he is better off staying back to give himself more time to see the ball. When you get eight to ten yards from a striker and he strikes it at your feet, what chance have you got? Not much of a chance when you are facing people like Greaves. They are ice-cool, like assassins. They stroke the ball past the keeper as if to say, "Well, what else did you expect me to do?" Whereas if people like me were to get into those positions, the ball might end up ten yards over the bar.

'I would say that seventy-five per cent of Greaves's goals were sidefooted. Whenever I think of Greaves, I immediately remember a Scotland–England under-21 match at Aberdeen when he was put through our defence and I was chasing him five or eight yards behind. It was always difficult to catch him in that situation because Jimmy could run almost as quickly with the ball as he could without it, and the ball was nearly always under total control by the way. He only had the keeper to beat, and as he shaped to hit the ball to one side and the keeper moved his bodyweight accordingly, Jimmy suddenly hit it just inches the wrong side of the keeper's other foot. As the ball went in, I thought, "You lucky bastard." But that was not right because over a period of some fifteen years I saw him do it time and time again.'

Another striker singled out by McLintock as being a cut above many others in the mental battleground of one-on-ones was Leeds United's Allan Clarke. He, too, achieved remarkable precision, something which clearly gave him enormous pride when he looked back on his career in an interview with me in 1996. 'I always remember the gaffer [Leeds manager Don Revie] saying to me, "If you have only one man to beat to get in a shot, Allan, just shake your body, go past him and do it. When you get into those positions, I know I can sit back and relax."

'The thing about my shooting was that I didn't let difficult angles worry me. Some people seem to look upon it almost as a crime for a keeper to be beaten on his near post, but I scored loads of near-post goals. More often than not I would hit the ball with the inside of my foot to get maximum accuracy, and I think a lot of keepers might have been taken by surprise at the power I was able to get into my shots. This came in particularly handy in one-against-one situations. As the keeper was moving towards me, I knew that there had to be a point at which he would have to stop, and I was quite happy to wait for that moment, even if it meant him getting quite close to me. As soon as he stopped, that was the moment I shot. Not only this, I hit the ball low and as close to the keeper as possible, knowing that he was going to struggle to get down to it quickly enough.

'Dave Harvey [the Leeds keeper] will tell you about things like that. I was only the third-choice penalty-taker at Leeds but I still used to practise taking them against Dave in training. Nine times out of ten I would hit the ball to a keeper's left if he was right-handed and vice versa. Dave was right-handed, and before I took penalties against him in training I actually told him where I was going to place the ball and he still couldn't stop them. He would then position himself increasingly further towards that post, and eventually he was so close to it that he could almost touch it. Even then I scored more than I missed.'

One obvious potential pitfall for strikers in one-on-one situations in open play concerns the difficulty of switching into the lower gear necessary to give them the right degree of composure. 'It's about accelerating to get through a defence and then suddenly decelerating to give yourself the calmness needed to stick the ball past the keeper,' said Andy Roxburgh. 'It [scoring] has to be easier if you are not trying to do it at a hundred miles an hour.' One illustration of that point, Roxburgh added, was the Ronaldo goal that brought Brazil their 1–0 win over Turkey in the 2002 World Cup semi-final. 'Of the strikers in England, Thierry Henry and Michael Owen are particularly good examples as well,' he went on. But what made that Ronaldo goal even more interesting to Roxburgh was the sudden toe-poke with which the outrageously gifted Brazilian produced as the finishing touch. It was a weak shot (if one could truly call it that), but then the nonchalant, subtle manner of the toe-ender – no more than a prod, with hardly any backlift and no follow-through – made it difficult to see how the Turkish keeper could have anticipated it.

In terms of the shooting instructions laid down in traditional football coaching manuals, the toe-poke is hardly textbook stuff, as Roxburgh pointed out. 'A lot of the old coaching books tell you that you must not toe-poke the ball. But as far as I'm concerned you can put them all in a bag and throw them in the bin.' He explained that such shots are commonplace in 'Futsal de Salon', the indoor five-a-side game that originated in South America and which has been a big factor in the development of many Brazilian stars. Roxburgh, added: 'It is easier to control the ball in futsal [than in a conventional eleven-a-side match] because the ball they use is heavier and does not bounce so much. As the ball hits you, it "dies". It's great for developing techniques such as lifting the ball over defenders and keeping it away from them with the sole of the foot. It's the same with those toe-poked shots: they just stub their toe at the ball and it flies.' Ronaldo himself attributed that goal against Turkey to his futsal experience. 'Nobody expected me to do it,' he said. 'It is a difficult technique, but it was just instinctive, and I owe it to playing a lot of futsal when I was younger.'

But there have also been some excellent demonstrations of the skill from non-futsal players. Roxburgh vividly remembers one from his days as Scotland coach, when Pat Nevin scored against the USA, by playing a one-two with Brian McClair on the edge of the penalty area and toe-poking a shot that went into the top corner of the net. 'People said, "Oh, it wasn't a proper shot, it was only a toe-ender," but Pat had actually been practising hitting the ball in this way at Everton. Apparently, Neville Southall [Everton's goalkeeper] had told him, "I hate toe-tenders because I can't read them," so Pat started producing them against him in training.'

Coincidentally, the day after my conversation with Roxburgh on this aspect of forward play I found Mark McGhee encouraging his strikers to try the toe-poke technique in a Millwall training session. 'Micky Quinn [McGhee's former Newcastle colleague] was great at it. Helped by his strong ankles and calves, he toe-ended more goals than any player I have seen. In a crowded penalty box, it must be an advantage for a striker to be able to get in his shot half a second earlier.'

One would think that it must also be an advantage for any striker to have a coach attending to his needs and requirements as closely as Dave Alred does with Jonny Wilkinson. But in soccer, the idea that the striker's role is almost as much a specialist position as that of goalkeeping, and thus requires specialist coaching, has not caught on as much as one might imagine. Goalkeeping coaches have become quite common, but the number of expert coaches for the exclusive use of the men at the front end of the team – the sharp end, as they like to describe it – is limited.

The biggest name among the specialist striking coaches is Ian Rush at Liverpool, but perhaps even more interesting is the England Rugby Union-style coaching and training set-up in which Beswick is involved at Middlesbrough. Boro's manager, Steve McClaren, has not gone as far as Sir Clive Woodward, whose backroom staff for England's triumphant 2004 World Cup campaign in Australia included not only Alred but also tackling, scrummage and line-out coaches. Still, McClaren, who like Woodward is happy to explore all manner of sports science avenues to maximise his team's performances and has clearly been influenced by the departmental coaching approach in American football, does have a goalkeeping coach (Jim Barron), a defensive coach (Keith Harrison) and an attacking coach (Steve Round). Some might argue that the benefits of the latter were hard to detect in Boro's unimpressive overall scoring record in the 2003/04 season. On the other hand, though, they did not have the best of luck with injuries, and their attack – featuring Gaizka Mendieta and Boudewijn Zenden on the flanks and that Brazilian bag of tricks Juninho feeding off Joseph Desiré-Job in the middle – did help bring them the League Cup, their first ever trophy.

Steve Round is not a former striker; he was a Derby County right-back or right-side midfielder whose career was cut short by injury at the age of 22. By then he was already coaching at Derby's School of Excellence, and he was the club's reserve-team coach at the time he joined his former Pride Park colleagues McLaren and Beswick at Middlesbrough. Considering his background as a player, it seems strange that he should have been given so much responsibility for improving Boro's scoring ability, but he maintained that he has always been a keen student of the 'creative' side of the game. 'Coaching is not about showing someone how to do it [score] by demonstrating it,' he said. 'Coaching is about breaking it down and explaining it.' He admitted, however, that gaining the trust and support of the strikers in his group has not always been easy. 'Strikers are not the easiest of players to deal with,' he said. 'Dave Sexton [one of England's leading post-war coaching figures] summed it up once when he talked about the differences between defenders and forwards. He described defenders as being the game's "soldiers" in that if you say to them, "There's a big wall over there, get over it," they will reply, "How long have we got to do it?" He described goalscorers as the "artists", and said that if you were to give them the same instruction, their reply would be more likely to be, "Why?" or "How much money will I get?" or "What is the best way to do it?" They are strong-minded people and they want answers. We had an attacking player here who was incredibly difficult. The time and effort I had to put in with him to get a performance out of him, any kind of performance, was extraordinary.' But, thanks partly to the player–staff 'bonding' effect of a pre-season training camp in Spain, what Round had to offer became accepted more readily.

Boro's belief that scoring is a collective responsibility is reflected by the prominently positioned poster in their training-ground dressing room, which reminds each section of the team of the minimum goal target McClaren has set for it. Hence the insistence of Round and Beswick that it is important for them to work with all the attacking players as a group – the midfielders and strikers rather than just the strikers. 'Strikers have to integrate themselves into the team pattern, so if you are concentrating just on strikers and their finishing you're not really getting to the essence of the issue,' Round said. 'In the past there has been a coaching culture where you coach the team to defend and to win the ball, and then, when you have got it, you just go and play. We are trying to go into it a lot more deeply. So when we win the ball, how do we go and play? How do we create? How do we score? These are basically the questions we are trying to answer.'

As far as those goal targets are concerned, Round said, 'Once we have come up with criteria on how we believe they can be achieved, the next step is to have an open debate about it with the players.' When one striker was asked whether he could see any problems with what was being asked of him, he replied, 'I was seen as the star player at my previous club and was allowed to get away with whatever I wanted to. You cannot allow that to happen here – you must keep me on a tight rein.' Round said: 'That player can get sloppy in training,' Round said, 'and because of what he told me it gives me an excuse to really have a go at him. He will look at me angrily, but then I will make out that I am tightening a belt around my waist [to emphasise his need to get rid of his slackness] and off he goes, as focused as ever.'

Before the start of the 2003/04 season, each of the players in Round's group was given a 'job description' sheet outlining what Boro considered to be the most important aspects of his role. 'We try to make it as simple as possible so each player knows what is expected of him and how he is being evaluated,' Round explained. The list handed to the front men, entitled *The Requirements of a Striker*, read:

1. CHALLENGE/COURAGE
   Pressure defenders
   Take the ball
2. HOLD THE BALL
3. GET INTO THE BOX
   Skill
   Movement
   Freedom
4. CREATE A GOAL
5. SCORE A GOAL.

The last sentence stated: 'If I miss, I only think, "I will get the next one."'

The list, of course, covers all the stages often necessary for a striker to go through before he or another member of the team can get into a scoring position: his part in enabling his team to win the ball, to retain possession and move it further up the field, and to open up the opposing defence in their penalty area. The other way of looking at it is for it to be read from the bottom, but Round said, 'Though people argue that it does not matter what a striker does beforehand as long as he scores, I take the opposite view. I feel that by doing all the things we expect of him [physically and mentally] he is bound to get more scoring chances. We say to the strikers, "If you win the ball thirty-five yards from the goal then you only have thirty-five yards to go to score, whereas if you win the ball a hundred yards from goal you have a hundred yards to go to score. So be our first line of defence and last line of attack."'

'They cannot score in every game,' Beswick added, 'and there are times when coming off without scoring can be very depressing to them. Strikers are noted for being a bit sensitive and requiring a lot of support. That is where the list of requirements we give them can come in handy. If you can show them the plus-points in other aspects of their game, it does help.'

But all strikers prone to 'emotional static', so when they aren't scoring, it helps them even more if they have been born with thick skins.

CHAPTER FOUR
THE WEIGHT OF EXPECTATION

'When you aren't scoring, it's amazing
the little faults that creep into your game
without you being conscious of them.
You might think you're doing the same things
you did when you were scoring,
but that's not always the case.'

ADE AKINBIYI

THE WEIGHT OF EXPECTATION

Dion Dublin, who spent much of his time in the 2003/04 season as Aston Villa's centre-half, says that the striker role is the one he enjoys the most. Nobody will be surprised at this, given his love of scoring and his scoring record. But what is surprising is his other explanation: the fact that he finds it less stressful. 'As a central defender you are always anxious about making a mistake which might cost your team a goal,' he explained. 'You can't afford to allow your concentration to drop for a second. You are on edge virtually all the time; it's very wearying. I don't think this is as much the case if you are a striker. Your mental approach is a bit different. To get goals, you have to be relaxed.'

So do we perhaps make too much of the pressures under which strikers do their jobs at times? They certainly don't seem to affect Alan Shearer. He seems genuinely surprised when you question him on this. 'I think you have to believe that you are going to score,' he said. 'That is a lot of it – not hoping you are going to score, but expecting to do so. When you go through spells without scoring, you do think, "Well, when is the next one going to come?" But I have always felt that it cannot go on for ever, that the longer I go without scoring the closer I get to being successful again. I cannot say that I have ever been that worried about it. If you are a goalscorer, then you are a goalscorer. You will always score.'

'Great scorers, and especially ones in top teams, look upon a missed chance like a missed bus,' said Andy Roxburgh. 'Their attitude is, "Doesn't matter – there will be another one along soon." That is what makes them great strikers. As for the pressure on them to score, don't forget that almost all of them have been strikers since they were small boys, so they have become conditioned to it. For example, if you have ever been in a country like Norway and stood at the top of an Olympic ski jump, you will think, "How the hell can anyone compete in this event?" But then as you drive around the explanation is provided by the number of smaller jumps used by the youngsters. The Olympic guys have built themselves up for the big jumps since they were boys. I think the same applies to goalscorers. Obviously, strikers can lose confidence. But they don't allow it to drop easily. Their confidence is not as fragile as you might think. It can't be.'

Indeed, signs of a striker not being as confident as he should be can often be detected only by an expert. 'One thing strikers do when they are confident is that they shoot when they cannot see all the goal,' Mark McGhee pointed out. 'The ball is in the box, they quickly get it under control, and even though they might have defenders in front of them, whoosh, they have a shot. It's amazing how many times the ball goes straight through [past the keeper and into the net]. When they are less confident they are inclined to want to take an extra touch so they can see more of the target, which is something you cannot do in league football because as soon as you take that extra touch the gap has closed completely. We are only talking about split seconds, which means that if that happens, the crowd are likely to think that the chance was not good enough, but quite often it was.'

Players generally and strikers particularly do not often admit publicly to being affected by nerves. Strikers believe it is essential to be seen as 'strong'. As one told me, 'You don't give the opposition any reason to think they can intimidate you.' Even so, men such as Bill Beswick would have a field day with a lot of strikers. One wonders what Beswick would have made of the extraordinary stories behind Ronaldo's disappointing performance in Brazil's 3–0 defeat by France in the 1998 World Cup final. Some passages in the book *Ronaldo*, written by Wensley Clarkson, invited the view that the Brazilian icon, bearing the hopes of millions on his shoulders and suffering from injuries which had looked like ruling him out of the match, was on the verge of a nervous breakdown.

According to Clarkson, a member of the Brazilian squad revealed that Ronaldo 'was shaking with fear' during the build-up to the game. 'Ronaldo was sleeping in his hotel room [eight hours before the nine pm kick-off],' Clarkson wrote. 'His room-mate Roberto Carlos was listening to his Walkman when, he later claimed, he was disturbed by the muffled sound of Ronaldo apparently having some kind of fit. Ronaldo turned pale, began sweating profusely and then suffered convulsions, with his arms flexed and his hands misshapen by the nervous tension.'

Certainly Ronaldo, who had scored four goals in his previous World Cup matches in France, looked a pale shadow of his old self in that final. However, if the pressure really did get to him – the only other explanation was that he might have been suffering a reaction from the drugs he had been prescribed to ease his injuries – he presented a far different picture of himself with the way in which he got over the experience. He, of course, was the star of Brazil's 2002 World Cup triumph, scoring both goals in the 2–0 win over Germany in the final to bring his total for the competition in Japan and Korea to eight. Apart from being the top scorer in that tournament, his aggregate World Cup record of twelve goals put him level with his Brazilian idol, Pele.

In another book, *Full Time* by Tony Cascarino and Paul Kimmage, Cascarino gave arguably the most remarkable of all insights into the self-doubts that can affect strikers. To many of his colleagues, the former Aston Villa, Celtic, Chelsea and Republic of Ireland centre-forward was the life and soul of any party. But in a breathtakingly honest account of his career, Cascarino admitted that when he was on the field he was repeatedly haunted by an 'irritating voice' in his head reminding him of his faults and all the reasons that could prevent him from scoring. 'Think positive?' he wrote. 'Not me. I think negative. I have always been a negative person. I have always thought negative thoughts. For as long as I can remember, there has been a little voice in my head that highlights my weaknesses and undermines my confidence. When it comes to the art of shooting oneself in the foot, I am world class. I think too much during the games. Most players analyse their performance after a game. Not me; I do it all the wrong way: I think of how I am playing as I play. Three bad passes and I'm glancing at the touchline [looking for the signal for him to be substituted]. I've scored and played brilliantly one week, and gone out and been awful the next, purely because some negative thought has hijacked me.'

In terms of missed chances, it's difficult to think of any striker who has fluffed more in one match than Plymouth Argyle's Marino Keith did during his team's shock 2–1 FA Cup fourth-round replay defeat at Dagenham and Redbridge in the 2001/02 season. It was possibly one of the most embarrassing performances by a striker in recent seasons, although Paul Sturrock, who had made Keith one of his first signings as Plymouth manager, saw no reason why he should feel uncomfortable about the decision. Sturrock, who had seen his fellow Scot in action at his previous clubs, Dundee United, Falkirk and Livingston, told me: 'I knew that a lot of teams would come to Plymouth to defend, pack a lot of men in or around our penalty box, so I needed a striker who could operate effectively in that area. Marino is the type of striker who lives in the box, and I'm not sure that Falkirk and Livingston were able to give him the service he needed, especially when they stepped up the league scale. They would have had to defend a lot more. They would have been looking to draw the opposition forward and hit through-balls to him, but he is just not a through-ball striker. On the assumption that we would generally put teams under greater pressure, he was a striker I felt I could take a chance on.'

On the nightmare that Keith and Plymouth experienced at Dagenham and Redbridge – where he missed enough chances for two or three games, let alone one – Sturrock continued, 'I'm not sure that his self-belief was really up to what it usually is. Confidence is a big factor in scoring, a very big factor, and to varying degrees all strikers go through low-confidence spells. When they get a chance you can sense their minds telling them to take extra care, whereas in normal circumstances they don't think about it, they just do it. The difference can be very subtle. Sometimes, this can happen to them without their really being conscious of it, and I think it can be dangerous to even mention it to them. It is something I rarely do because I am always wary of making the psychological barrier bigger. If a striker has a run of matches when he is missing chances, it can be amazing how easily he can get back on to the right track. Just one goal, any type of goal, will do, and Marino is one of those strikers whom you would never bet against getting that turning point. Though he goes through spells when he cannot hit a barn door, any slight drop in his finishing confidence does not mean he will give up.

'In that match at Dagenham and Redbridge I think he missed something like nine chances. Most of his misses were in the first half, and even now people ask me, "Why did you not take him off?" It was simple: he was the only player creating chances. They were all dropping to him and I thought that sooner or later he was bound to stick one or two of them in.' Just as he did in a subsequent match at Queens Park Rangers, where he scored Plymouth's goal in a rare 3–1 defeat with a tremendous shot into the far corner of the net from the left. 'About five minutes before, he missed a good chance with a header – he didn't even hit the target – and then he struck a shot which I think hit the corner flag,' Sturrock continued. 'But there he was, trying his luck again from the same position. Sometimes you think, "What is he shooting from there for?" and then it's "Oh my God, what a goal!" That's the kind of striker he is.'

Apart from his mentality, Keith has possibly also been helped by the fact that his club and the level at which he has operated do not attract much media coverage. The newspaper and TV spotlight on his mistakes is nowhere near as broad and intense as it is on those of his counterparts in the Premiership or in international football. It is certainly nothing like the spotlight that fell on Gordon Smith after the Scot's miss for Brighton and Hove Albion in the 1983 FA Cup final against Manchester United – arguably the most famous of all the goal misses in English football.

When Smith was presented with his chance in the last minute of extra time, with his unfancied team holding United at 2–2, he was perhaps the last player one would have expected to make a mess of it. After all, Smith had played in six Scottish Cup finals for Rangers, and he had even scored the winner for them against Celtic in the 1978 Scottish League Cup final. He had also opened the scoring for Brighton at Wembley, with a header. Thus, when Brighton's centre-forward Mick Robinson burst through the United defence and laid off the ball to an unmarked Smith ten yards out, the BBC Radio 2 match commentator, Peter Jones, had no hesitation in stating, 'And Smith must score!' Smith thought the same, with only the keeper Gary Bailey to beat, especially when Bailey dived to his left, leaving an inviting space for him to strike the ball into. But Smith hit the ball too low, propelling it against Bailey's leg. Bailey then denied Smith the chance to make amends from the rebound by pouncing on the loose ball and hugging it gratefully to his chest.

The match ended 2–2 and United went on to win the replay 4–0. Brighton, at the bottom of the First Division, were relegated. That, of course, was not Smith's fault. But had Brighton won the FA Cup, and thus qualified for the European Cup-Winners Cup, maybe some of the problems that followed their Wembley disappointment – especially the financial ones – might have been avoided. Inevitably, it was particularly difficult for them to wipe out the memory of that disappointment in the 1983/84 season, when their erratic results caused them to finish ninth.

This was not a good season for Smith at Brighton either. He made only eleven full and four substitute appearances for them in the league the following season, scoring just four goals (including two penalties). But then Billy McNeill signed him for Manchester City for £35,000, and he went on to get fifteen goals in 49 appearances for them. He ended his career in England with Oldham Athletic and played in Austria and Switzerland before retiring as a player and becoming assistant manager at St Mirren in 1988.

Smith, now working in Scotland as a financial consultant and a TV and radio pundit, has never been allowed to forget his Wembley nightmare. Those Jones words, 'And Smith must score!' – which became the title of the Brighton fanzine – are almost as famous as the Kenneth Wolstenholme BBC TV commentary ('They think it's all over – it is now') that accompanied Geoff Hurst clinching his World

Cup final hat-trick in 1966. Smith recalled a Manchester City club tour of Malaysia the following year, when a Chinese boy approached him for his autograph while he was soaking up the sun by the hotel swimming pool. 'You Gordon Smith?' the boy asked. 'How you miss that sitter in final?' 'It is all people ever want to talk to me about,' Smith said. 'I could make a cottage industry out of telling the story of what happened with me that day. Even now, hardly a day goes by without somebody mentioning that miss to me.'

However, his memories of it do go down well in his after-dinner speeches, and it is clear that the miss has not left him with any emotional scars. One reason, he explained, is that he wasn't really a striker. 'A lot of people have tended to overlook this. I remember an article in which Jimmy Case [his Brighton team-mate] recalled a Brighton fan bemoaning the fact that the FA Cup final chance had fallen to me, and Jimmy telling him, "Look, of all the players I have played with here, Gordon is the one I would have backed the most to score in that situation." I was quite chuffed by that because I was a midfield player. I only played up front in the cup final because we were short of strikers: Andy Ritchie had been transferred to Leeds in a part-exchange deal involving Terry Connor, and Connor couldn't play at Wembley because he was cup-tied. I was not a recognised striker at Manchester City either, even in the season when I was their joint top scorer [1984/85]. I was actually operating as a wide left midfielder.

'The miss might have had an adverse effect on me if I had been a young, inexperienced player, but I was twenty-eight then; I had a good understanding of what I was all about as a player and a person and I was mature enough to be able to put my experiences in football, the good and the bad, into their proper perspective. Obviously I was disappointed over the miss, for myself, the team and the supporters. But I cannot honestly say that I went to pieces over it.'

THE WEIGHT OF EXPECTATION

Smith's point about being more of a midfielder than a striker could also be used in defence of Geoff Thomas. He, too, is famous for missing a chance most believed he should have taken with his eyes shut, and it happened in his one and only England appearance, against France at Wembley in 1991. He had only the goalkeeper to beat but produced a shot that almost hit the corner flag. And, of course, no list of glaring England misses would be complete without the one perpetrated by the late Jeff Astle in the 1970 World Cup quarter-final against Brazil in Mexico, when the popular West Brom centre-forward, brought on as a substitute, reacted to a panic-stricken Brazilian defender heading the ball straight to his feet by blasting it over an open goal. England were a goal down at the time, and that's the way it remained. The possibility that Astle might have been suffering from 'emotional static' seemed to be lost on the England players as they debated the incident around their hotel swimming pool the following day. 'How was it possible for Jeff to miss a chance like that?' Alan Ball asked. As it happened, Ball should have known the answer because Astle had earlier provided him with a good chance by getting his head to a high cross, only for Ball to waste it.

The England striker who has suffered the biggest credibilty problems in recent seasons is Emile Heskey. Few international strikers have been subjected to greater media criticism than Heskey, whose struggle to assert himself as a scorer for Liverpool as well as Sven-Goran Eriksson's team led to his being transferred to Birmingham in May 2004. Among those who have also found it difficult to shine under the microscope of an entire country is John Aldridge. He said that the Republic of Ireland team he played for was the only one in which he suffered what he described as 'a mental scoring block'. He did not score in any of his first nineteen international matches – by far the longest non-scoring run of his entire career and one that coincided, strangely, with his emergence as a top-class player with Liverpool. Aldridge reckons it was partly due to the Republic of Ireland's tactics under Jack Charlton. He put a big emphasis on turning opposing defenders with passes hit deep into the space behind their full-backs – the 'corners', as coaches describe it, and Aldridge says: 'In that system, I was a runner not a goalscorer. I would be the one chasing the ball into the corners.' He admits, though, that he might have taken Charlton's instructions too far at times and that the longer he went without scoring the bigger that mental block became. 'When I did get chances, I was hitting the woodwork, they were getting cleared off the line – I was missing sitters, really. I didn't want to admit it publicly at the time, but deep down I knew I wasn't as confident as I was at club level. Had I been an England player, I don't think I would have lasted very long: the media would have hounded me out after five or six games. I have a lot to thank Jack for, because he kept faith in me. He felt I was pivotal to the system he wanted to play, so the more the Irish media said he shouldn't play me the more he dug his heels in.'

Aldridge eventually broke his duck in the 4–0 win over Tunisia in Dublin in October 1989. He got the last goal thanks to the spirit of generosity in Ray Houghton, who passed up a scoring opportunity for himself to lay one on a plate for Aldridge. 'I think he probably felt sorry for me,' Aldridge said. Not long afterwards he moved to Real Sociedad in Spain where his experience of being used as a lone striker against teams using man-for-man marking systems, not to mention his exposure to a more disciplined lifestyle, helped take his game on to a different level. 'The Real Sociedad system rotated around me and was mostly about manipulating teams into certain positions in order to give me the final ball. My spell in Spain taught me a lot about when to run the corners and when not to.'

Aldridge ended his international career with a total of nineteen goals from 69 matches. It put him joint second on their list of all-time international scorers with Don Givens, just one goal behind Frank Stapleton.

In all the time it had taken him to get off the mark, the one saving grace for Aldridge, outside his general work for the team, was that at least the Republic of Ireland were getting goals from others. This did not happen for Northern Ireland, whose run of thirteen matches without a goal from March 2002 to October 2003 – a European international record and also a world one if one takes into account that the precise time figure for their failure to score was 1,298 minutes – was particularly agonising to their Preston striker David Healy. True, Northern Ireland are the weakest of the four national United Kingdom teams, and Healy often found himself toiling up front on his own. However, he was recognised as their best striker and he did get some good chances in that depressing run, notably during the 1–0 defeat in Armenia in March 2003, when sympathy for him over the tremendous shot the keeper managed to touch on to the woodwork was offset by disappointment with his failure to get in a close-range header with the goal at his mercy.

All this seemed difficult to understand when one looked at the start of Healy's international career. He had just been loaned to Port Vale by Manchester United when he made his international debut against Luxembourg in February 2000, and in fact had made only one appearance in senior football up to that point (for United in a League Cup tie at Aston Villa four months earlier). Nonetheless, he scored twice in a 3–1 Irish victory, and over the rest of his spell at Port Vale he took his international goal ratio to three in three matches. It became five in seven after his return to Old Trafford, and following his transfer to Preston in December 2000 (initially on loan) it was extended to a highly respectable eight in fifteen matches.

He had made a good start at Preston, too, with ten goals in his

26 matches in the 2000/01 season, thus summing up why the club had paid £1.5 million for him in January. But the season ultimately produced disappointment for Preston: they were beaten in the First Division promotion play-off final by Bolton, and Healy's star seemed on the wane the following season. At the time of his eighth Northern Ireland goal in the 1–0 win over Malta in October 2001, Healy's record for his club was one in twelve games, and he was able to add only nine more (including a hat-trick against Stockport County) in his remaining 37 matches.

It seemed clear that Healy, in his early twenties, had begun to suffer a mental and physical backlash from the excitement of his early successes. Indeed, a few weeks before the end of the season, with Kelham O'Hanlon installed as Preston's caretaker-manager following the departure of David Moyes to Everton, Healy was displaced in the starting line-up by Clyde Wijnhard. 'Clyde is a big striker,' Healy said, 'and Kelham opted for a style of play that was more direct. It didn't really suit me – I prefer the ball into feet – but I couldn't really complain about it because Clyde did quite well and I was low on confidence anyway.'

Healy's anxiety that another Preston manager might not rate him as highly as Moyes had done seemed to be borne out when Craig Brown, appointed Moyes's successor at the end of the season, opted for Ricardo Fuller (his summer signing from Hearts) and Richard Cresswell as his first-choice strikers. Even after Fuller's serious injury that October, Healy was kept largely on the periphery of the first-team action.

But Northern Ireland, woefully short of striking options, continued to play him – which was part of his problem in that non-scoring run. 'I was thankful to Sammy McIlroy [the manager] for sticking by me, but maybe that was the wrong thing to do because when you are short of confidence at club level you are bound to take it on to the international stage,' Healy argued. 'My early success probably hindered me a bit. Initially, everything is new: teams don't know much about you and you are full of adrenalin. But then people start expecting you to score in every game, which is difficult for a striker in a top team let alone one that doesn't create many chances. Also, you have to bear in mind that maybe six or seven of my games for Ireland [during their run without scoring] came at times when I was not playing for Preston's first team. I was playing for the reserves, but that was to keep my fitness up more than anything. I think most players find it difficult to be totally focused in reserve-team football; I know I did. In terms of giving me a competitive edge, I wasn't getting as much out of it as I needed. In international football, there are games in which you might only get six touches of the ball and only one half chance – a twenty-yard shot or something like that. So you have to be in that zone.'

Healy was able to get back into it with Preston in the 2003/04 season following a less than spectacular loan spell at Norwich City, because of a slight change in roles. Brown told me, 'I like my mainline striker to have a lot of pace, and I'm not sure that David is quick enough for that. Unlike people such as Fuller, he cannot outrun defenders. But he can beat them with trickery, and he is an excellent striker of the ball, so we have played him off the main striker. Being deeper means he gets a bit more attacking freedom. He tends to come forward mainly from the right, because whenever the opposition win the ball it's his job to shuttle across and cut off their left-back. His attacking ability from that sort of area is excellent.'

Brown has certainly been impressed with Healy's shooting. 'He is possibly the finest striker of a ball I have worked with,' he said. 'I love the way he clips the ball. With such a short backlift, he surprises you with the power he gets into his shots. Our players marvel at some of the goals he gets in training and matches.' Brown's favourite was Healy's winning goal in Preston's 2–1 victory at West Ham in January 2004. 'He was about fourteen yards out when the ball was cut back to him from a corner, and he hit the ball first-time, without appearing to really set up his body shape for it. He actually put spin on it, and the ball went under David James's body.'

But it was with his head that Healy ended his Northern Ireland nightmare, against Norway at Windsor Park the month following that West Ham tie. With McIlroy having resigned as manager to join Stockport County (how was that for an indictment on the state of his national team?) and having been replaced by Lawrie Sanchez, the Irish suffered another humiliating defeat. However, you could understand why the dismay over the four goals they conceded was cast aside to some extent by Healey's fifty-sixth-minute headed goal from Keith Gillespie's cross. It was his first Northern Ireland goal in fifteen matches, and what made it doubly exciting for him was that his international total of nine put him level in the all-time scorers' list with two Irish soccer legends, George Best and Norman Whiteside, and only four behind Colin Clarke at the top.

It was a breakthrough that could have been anticipated in the light of the change in his fortunes at Preston. He hadn't scored in any of their opening eleven matches, but by the time he faced Norway he had got ten in eighteen. The upsurge in his confidence was again seen in Northern Ireland's next match, against Estonia in Tallinn at the end of March, when he scored his most spectacular goal at international level with a wonderful strike from twenty yards. And he should have got another in that game: he reacted quickly to the rebound from a blocked shot by Jeff Whitley but fired the ball over the bar from six yards. But he was easily forgiven by the Irish faithful because the chance he did take meant their team won 1–0 – their first victory in sixteen games.

THE WEIGHT OF EXPECTATION

It also happened to be quite a good season for Stoke City's much-travelled and much-maligned Ade Akinbiyi. It's difficult to think of any striker who has received the amount of stick from fans that he has. It's also difficult to think of any striker who can provide a better example of the thin line between success and failure for such men, and the speed with which they can make the jump from hero to zero and back to hero again.

Though cynics might suggest that the case of Akinbiyi is a perfect example of how desperate clubs can be to get goalscorers, and the mistakes they can make as a result, it's not difficult to see why they have been attracted to him. The Nigerian, big, strong and exceptionally quick, cuts a dynamic figure in the athletic sense. Indeed, as a schoolboy growing up in Hackney, east London, he could easily have joined Arsenal, but as his parents wanted to move to Norfolk he plumped for Norwich City. Although he struggled to establish himself there, he went on to make an increasingly big name for himself at Gillingham (28 league goals in 68 matches), Bristol City (21 in 47) and Wolves (16 in 37). Indeed, his progress was reflected by the transfer fees handed out for him: Gillingham had only paid Norwich £25,000 for him, but Bristol City signed him for a club-record £1.2 million, Wolves for a club-record £3 million, and then Leicester brought him on to the Premiership stage for a club-record £5 million. So much for the rise of Akinbiyi. The fall was illustrated by Leicester selling him to Crystal Palace for £2.2 million and then Stoke taking him off Palace's hands on a free transfer.

It was at Leicester, where Akinbiyi looked ill at ease in the Premiership and the pressure on him to save his team from relegation, that his image took its biggest battering. He managed only eleven goals in 58 league matches, and he was in no position to complain about not having had enough chances. Leicester fans still wince over the memory of his hatful of glaring misses during the televised 4–1 home defeat by Liverpool in October 2001, especially the one where his attempt to head the ball in from a few yards out ended with it hitting him on the shoulder and going wide.

Shortly afterwards, Opta, the Premiership's official statisticians, revealed that as many as 83 per cent of Akinbiyi's shots that season had been off target. This was highlighted by the *Sun* newspaper, which ran a prominent story describing Akinbiyi as 'the worst striker in the league'. Mark Irwin, the writer, suggested that Peter Taylor, the manager who had signed him from Leicester and who had subsequently been replaced by Dave Bassett, might have lost his job because of the striker's wayward finishing. 'Leicester fans are wondering why their club forked out £5 million for a guy who cannot hit a cow's backside with a banjo,' he wrote. By this stage the Leicester fans had turned against Akinbiyi – to the point where a Leicester supporters' spokesman admitted that the striker's fallibility had become an 'obsession' with them. Micky Adams, then Leicester's assistant manager, said, 'We just have to relax him more. I have told him that whatever is troubling him, let me worry about it during a match. It's not easy when 22,000 fans are booing, but he needs to clear his mind.'

But the tag of being the worst striker in the game continued to prove a heavy psychological millstone around his neck, even when he moved back to the Nationwide League to join Crystal Palace. It seemed a big compliment to Akinbiyi that he was signed for Palace by a former striker as accomplished as Trevor Francis. But Palace's fans, brainwashed by Akinbiyi's Leicester image, did not give him much of a chance to show them it was justified. Akinbiyi, not helped at Palace by his injury problems either, attracted negative vibes even when Steve Kember, Francis's successor as manager, froze him out of the first-team picture and put him up for sale. Reports indicated that, though other clubs were interested in him, they were put off by

Akinbiyi's unwillingness to accept a drop – or at least a major one – in the salary Palace were paying him. The inference to be drawn from all this was that Akinbiyi was putting money before professional pride and ambition, and that Palace, struggling financially, were being held to ransom.

Nonetheless, Francis is still saddened by the memory of Akinbiyi's treatment at the hands of the Palace fans. 'In more than thirty years in professional football I have never experienced anything quite like it,' he said. 'It was absolutely savage, and I have nothing but admiration for the way he handled it. It's one thing getting stick from the media, but when you are on the pitch as a professional footballer and can hear supporters from both sides laughing at you – that's what was happening to him. He is a smashing fellow. He was very well liked by the other Palace players and he worked tremendously hard, yet our own supporters were laughing at everything he attempted to do, ridiculing him. I have always said to my players that I will back them as long as they give me a hundred per cent. That's what the supporters expect as well, so I found it rather strange that Ade, who could not be faulted in his general effort at all, was subjected to that sort of stick. It's cruel.'

Francis can easily understand why Leicester signed him. 'He is very pacey and he is constantly looking to get in behind defenders,' he explained. 'He's a good player to have in any team because he turns opponents and stretches defences. The downside is that he is not a particularly clinical finisher. If you had come to watch some of his training sessions at Palace, you probably would have thought, "How has this player scored the goals that he has?" He's not what I would call a clean striker of the ball; he can often be a very scruffy striker of the ball. But I think this is offset by his ability to get into scoring positions.' Echoing the point that Paul Sturrock made about Marino Keith, Francis continued, 'It is essential for strikers to be able to anticipate where the ball is going to go. Not all of them do. Occasionally, when I'm watching what a striker does when the ball comes across the box or is played through, I'm thinking, "Why hasn't he reacted to that?" Usually the reason is that he hasn't a good enough understanding of the game; he hasn't been able to anticipate the situation. He just does not see it. It is different with Akinbiyi – that's what he's really good at. OK, he might miss more chances than other strikers, but then this is possibly because he gets into the positions to miss more often than them.'

Francis's assertion that Akinbiyi did not deserve to be treated so harshly by the Leicester and Crystal Palace fans is quickly underlined when you meet him. He seems smaller than he looks on the field, and is surprisingly reserved and quietly spoken. Initially he comes across almost as shy, but then as the publicity he has been given has caused him to think twice about granting media interview requests it's tempting to put that down to caution.

How else has the criticism affected him?

'I'm a Christian, which I think helps a lot,' Akinbiyi told me, 'and I have had a lot of support from my family and friends. I have my own little world, and the people in it are the only ones who really matter to me. I don't go any further than that. The other thing that has kept me going is that I love football. I came from nowhere to be a professional footballer; in fact, for some time when I was a boy I wasn't that keen on playing football. I was very much into athletics at school and, if anything, I wanted to be an athlete. Then, all of a sudden, my teacher sort of bullied me into playing football and it all mushroomed from there. So every time I'm on a downer, I think, "Look how far you have come."'

I tell him about Francis's comments concerning his anticipation.

'There are a lot of things to it,' he said. 'Some of it is gambling.

If a centre-half looks like he's going to get the ball, you have to think that he's going to miss it. That's what I was taught as a youngster – you have to gamble. As a kid, you tend to run about just for the sake of it, but if you want to progress you have to think about what you are doing and you have to have players who are going to see what you are doing. This was one of the main reasons for my success at Bristol City. Brian Tinnion [City's highly respected left-side midfielder] has one of the best left foots I have ever seen. Every time he had the ball he knew where I was going and I knew where he was going to put it. I would say that almost all of my goals at City were created by that left foot of his. But generally, there is a frustrating side to it in that a lot of the runs you make go unnoticed by the crowd. You can spend the whole ninety minutes running around, getting into positions to receive the ball, but it's usually only when you score that they notice.'

And also when you miss?

'That's right. One problem for me [with finishing] is that because I'm naturally quick I want to do everything quick. I admit that sometimes I rush things unnecessarily. The manager says to me, "When you get there [into a scoring situation], that's when you need to relax and shut out everything." But occasionally it's difficult for someone like me to get into that state, especially in one-against-one situations where you have so much time. Then you fail to score, and the crowd are thinking, "He gets tons of money and he has missed an opportunity like that," as if it was something you meant to do. All that has happened is that it has not gone right for you, which happens to everybody in every walk of life.

'When you aren't scoring, it's amazing the little faults that creep into your game without you being conscious of them. You might think you're doing the same things you did when you were scoring, but that's not always the case. I keep a lot of videos and DVDs of my matches, and as I was watching one the other day I saw something which surprised me a bit. When the ball was played up to me, and I laid it off, I noticed that I had had more time to turn with the ball than I had thought. I got kidded by the defender, who had touched me on the back as the ball was being played to me to make me think that I wasn't going to be able to turn with the ball, and then dropped back five yards. I hadn't been aware of that at the time.'

Now, he can also see why he didn't do better at Leicester. Referring to his lack of experience of playing in high-pressure matches in front of big crowds, he said, 'I probably didn't spend long enough at Wolves. It was only ten months, but if I could turn back the clock I would have wanted it to be two or three years. It's a big club, and staying there would have helped me develop more. But I cannot really have any excuses for what happened to me at Leicester. I blame myself because I took too much for granted and relied too much on people pushing me. The standard in the Premiership is so much higher than it is in the Nationwide, and you cannot expect to adjust just like that. I worked exceptionally hard at Gillingham and Bristol City: I did a lot of extra training at both clubs, and also at Wolves. But when I got to Leicester I found that there was no one to do extra training with. I should have said, "OK, you will have to take the initiative and do it yourself." But for some reason – maybe because I was in the Premiership and felt that I had arrived – I did not have the motivation. That's the habit I got into. Peter Taylor did eventually try and rectify this, but by that time I think I had lost it.

'Generally, the crowd at Leicester didn't bother me that much. Even the article in the *Sun* didn't really upset me. The first I knew about it was when my brother telephoned me that morning and said, "Don't get the *Sun*." Well, I did, and I had a right giggle over it. It appeared the day before the match against Sunderland, when I scored my first league goal of the season [to give Leicester a 1–0 win]. They were saying, "The worst striker in England scored." You had to see the funny side of it.

'As a professional footballer you are going to get criticised no matter what. I have had criticism even when I have been playing well. It's not pleasant, but you appreciate that if you can't take it you shouldn't be in the game. What really made me sick at Leicester, though, was that during a match against Liverpool my brother told me that a guy sitting behind him – somebody who was working for Leicester and who I got on well with – was absolutely slaughtering me. I challenged him about it the next day. "You were shouting abuse at me," I said. "Yeah," he said, "but I'd had too much to drink." Which was no excuse as far as I was concerned. From that day onwards I took extra care in deciding who my friends were. It made me better, stronger.'

But he still needed his colleagues to show faith in him. 'The crowd might have been on my back at Leicester, but the good thing for me was that all the boys [the other Leicester players] stuck by me. All players give each other stick in training and the dressing room, but when I was going through my worst periods, they were like my family.' And he certainly needed the public backing he was given by Peter Taylor and Trevor Francis. 'The support of the manager is the main thing,' Akinbiyi said. 'When you are going through a bad time, it's great to have a manager who will stand up for you and say, "I know this boy, I know what he can do." No matter how mentally strong they are, I think all strikers would agree that this is important to them.'

No manager has shown as much faith in Akinbiyi as Stoke City's Tony Pulis, who was also the manager who signed him for Gillingham and Bristol City. Such is the rapport they have established it seems unlikely that Akinbiyi would have been able to adopt a laid-back attitude to improving his game at Leicester had Pulis been there. As Akinbiyi said, 'He is a manager who is in your face. He even likes to know what you eat, what you do at home, things like that. It can be irritating, but I don't mind because he wants you to do well.' Pulis nodded in agreement. 'You have to keep on at him and push him,' he said. 'He's a lad who needs attention and I probably spend more time talking to him than I do with a lot of the other players. Some players need a little bit of tender care more than others – we are all different, aren't we? – and Ade is probably one of them. But it's not all about kisses and cuddles. He does react to people who are straight and honest with him, so the occasional kick up the backside, at the right time, is OK with him as well.

'If there is one thing that I have kept on at him about, it's the importance of him concentrating on his strengths. Some managers and coaches have a strange attitude to goalscorers as far as I'm concerned: they're inclined to talk to them more about what they can't do than what they can do. Ade is not a ball-player. His greatest attributes are his pace, power and anticipation, so getting the best out of him is all about simplifying things for him and getting him to get right up on to the shoulders of opposing defenders and find scoring positions. I get annoyed with him sometimes when he moves deep and plays in front of defenders. When we were at Gillingham, it prompted me to give him the biggest rollicking he has ever had from me. In the first half he was pussyfooting around like you would not believe. I really tore into him at half-time, so much so that his neck puffed up and his eyes were glaring at me as if he was about to throttle me. In the second half he scored two fantastic goals. "I meant what I said," I told him. "You are not a pussyfooting player, you are a dynamic player, and you will only score goals by exploiting that." Maybe this aspect of his game was lost at Leicester. Most Premiership players are skilful on the ball, and maybe Ade felt that he had to be the same as them. I don't know. All we have really done here is to encourage him to concentrate on his strengths and show him that we value him.'

Pulis initially signed Akinbiyi on loan at the end of March 2003, with Stoke fourth from bottom in the First Division. He scored his first goal for them in his third match, a 2–1 win over Wimbledon, but it was in his fourth on the last day of the season that his Leicester and Palace memories were put firmly behind him. The only remaining First Division relegation issue still not settled by then concerned the last drop-zone position and the battle between Stoke and Brighton to avoid it. Stoke had to win at home to Reading to stay up at Brighton's expense, whereas a Stoke defeat and a Brighton victory at Grimsby would have meant the reverse.

Stoke seemed to have the tougher task because although Reading had already clinched promotion they had one of the best defensive records in the country and their manager, Alan Pardew, was a close friend of his Brighton counterpart, Steve Coppell. Though he wasn't aware of it, Akinbiyi took a leaf from the psychological 'creative visualisation' book on his car journey to the Stoke ground. He recalled, 'As I was driving through Stoke, I put the radio on. It's something I don't usually do before a game, but I was so excited about this match. It was amazing because I immediately heard a guy talking about the match and saying something like, "Wouldn't it be a great boost for Akinbiyi if he were to score the winning goal?" It gave me a good feeling, and I kept visualising it.'

As it happened, a winning goal for Stoke didn't matter because Brighton were beaten 2–1. But the Stoke fans could not have known that when, after 55 minutes' play, Akinbiyi gleefully dispatched a Lewis Neal cross into the net with a header.

Zero to hero? Akinbiyi, who was signed by Stoke permanently

that summer, hardly had a scoring record in the Henry category in the 2003/04 season (ten goals in 23 league matches). However, in view of that goal against Reading, few Stoke fans were quibbling with the fact that the number 10 jersey – famous in other countries as the one donned by a team's star player – had been allocated to him. One Stoke supporter even initiated a website in honour of Akinbiyi. His introductory message reads: 'As an avid Stoke supporter, I can safely say that my favourite player is Ade Akinbiyi. This is a site to show the world that Ade Akinbiyi is no longer a joke and all those negative connotations he has carried with him are well and truly in the past. He has quickly become a cult hero among Stoke supporters and this site is a sign of our appreciation of a player I can well and truly call a Stoke City hero. For all those Leicester and Crystal Palace fans reading this, you must have had bad managers because Ade is certainly The Man here at Stoke.'

CHAPTER FIVE
LORDS OF THE MANOR

'You could say I was a tad demanding.
I would think that any striker worth
his salt has to be.'
STEVE ARCHIBALD

Arsenal manager Arsène Wenger has mixed feelings about the age-old view that goalscorers need to be selfish and greedy. To Wenger, the best strikers play for their teams, not themselves. Despite the importance of their jobs, they have no problem with helping colleagues in other departments do theirs; and when they get a scoring chance, they are quite happy to set up someone else for a goal if he happens to be in a better position. As Wenger said, this point is perfectly illustrated by Arsenal's Thierry Henry.

In helping his defence, Henry is not quite in the same class as Ian Rush, whose willingness to do a lot of running off the ball up front just to make it difficult for opposing defenders to start attacking moves led to the view that he was Liverpool's best defender, let alone goalscorer. But Henry still does his bit at Arsenal. He is no strolling player. In addition to his high number of goals, he also happens to have one of the best Premiership records for goal-assists.

After Henry's performance in setting up the Robert Pires and Freddie Ljungberg goals that gave Arsenal their 2–0 European Champions League win over Lokomotiv Moscow in December

2003, putting the Gunners through to the last sixteen of the competition, Wenger said, 'Lokomotiv were organised to give him no room at all, yet he found the space to make others score. That is an area where he has improved a lot. Football suffers from selfishness in front of goal. For me the complete player is the player who gives the ball when it has to be given in the final third. People are too forgiving of players who want to score goals to the point where it is an obsession. Those players try to score from all manner of angles and, because of their persistence, they finally get one. But they have killed ten chances on the way. Those players will say, "The team lost 2–1, but at least I scored." However, I do not think that is something to be proud of. I have as much respect for the player who plays the final ball as I have for the goalscorer.'

But, as Wenger added, Henry is arguably the most gifted all-round forward in the world. The terms of reference for most other strikers have to be narrower.

The extent to which they should be expected to concentrate on their basic responsibility has always been something of a grey area. Graeme Sharp recalled, 'When Howard Kendall [his manager at Everton] pointed out to me that I hadn't been scoring, I would say, "But my general play is OK – I'm making chances for other players." But his reaction was, "Yeah, your general play is good, but at the end of the day people judge you on your scoring record." I must admit that there were times when I allowed all the compliments about my play as a target man to go to my head. I started believing my own publicity and probably did not get into scoring positions as much as I could and should have done. But unselfishness was looked upon as one of my strengths.'

To varying degrees, all strikers argue that it is important for them to remain mentally and physically sharp to be able to apply the finishing touches to attacking moves and that this cannot be achieved if they are devoting too much energy to other aspects of the game. But with teams being forced to become more fluid tactically, in terms of outfield players interchanging positions and being able to do different jobs, and the game as a whole becoming so geared to fitness and physical power, the concept of strikers only needing to truly come alive inside the penalty area (or in some cases the six-yard box) is now seen as an increasingly difficult luxury to justify.

Preston's Craig Brown, the former Scotland coach, recalled that none of the strikers he played with at Dundee and Rangers had greater skill, and less desire to do more than stick the ball in the net, than Alan Gilzean at Dundee. 'He stayed up the field and his pants were always immaculate. In the last fifteen minutes of a game, when most of the other players were tired, he was as fresh as a daisy. He scored a lot of goals towards the end of games, but the days when strikers could isolate themselves from the other aspects of the game have gone.'

Those who have been perceived as having done so include Jimmy Greaves, the greatest of all scorers in top-flight football in England since the war. But Greaves's image as just a brilliant finisher – a so-called 'goal-poacher' who was generally hardly seen in the build-up – hardly does him justice. He created the opportunities for a number of his goals virtually on his own, occasionally with mazy dribbles through a defence from the halfway line. He scored one such goal on his Chelsea debut at Tottenham, at the age of seventeen. In the famous photograph of it, taken from behind the Tottenham goal, was best summed up by the expression of bewilderment on the face of one of the Tottenham defenders who had been left on their backsides in their attempts to stop him taking the ball past them. The experience of seeing that goal is one of my most cherished football memories as a schoolboy. Another personal favourite was a similarly individualistic Greaves goal for Spurs against Leicester

City, when he just managed to stop a long clearance from the Spurs keeper, Pat Jennings, from going out of play on the right touchline, then beat three Leicester defenders and finally the Leicester keeper, Peter Shilton, before slipping the ball into an empty net.

Greaves, though, did personify the unwillingness of outstanding scorers to do a lot of running off the ball in general play – a characteristic that ultimately rebounded against him in the 1966 World Cup finals. The fact that a scoring genius such as Greaves, having lost his England place for the quarter-final against Argentina through injury, wasn't able to get back into the side at the expense of his replacement Geoff Hurst or Roger Hunt provided as good an example as any of the demand for strikers to broaden their contribution to teams. Sir Alf Ramsey's belief that Hurst and Hunt would be better suited to his 4–4–2 system was proved right by England's 4–2 win and, of course, Hurst's achievement in becoming the first player ever to score a World Cup final hat-trick. Even so, his decision to leave Greaves out was one he never fully lived down. Even now it tends to be viewed among Greaves's admirers as some kind of insult against the little maestro and the extraordinary scoring standards he represented.

Of all the top-class strikers of the modern era who could be described as singing from a different hymn sheet to that of their colleagues, Gerd Müller, the Bayern Munich and West Germany star of the 1970s, must be at or close to the top of the list. 'Der Bomber', as he was called, did not need to do much more than apply the finishing touch to his team-mates' work, mainly because the other nine outfield players had more than enough ability to dominate the opposition. And that was just as well, because Müller, who did not cut the most impressive of athletic figures with his short, stocky build, and whose basic ball skills were comparatively limited, would almost certainly have been a liability to them had he been asked to do more.

Looking nothing like a great footballer was a cross Müller had to bear from the very start of his career at the top. Legend has it that when he moved to Bayern in 1963, their coach, 'Tshik' Cajkovski, told the club president, 'I'm not putting this bear among our racehorses.' When it came to taking chances inside the penalty box, though, Müller proved himself a thoroughbred. Looking scruffy and unfit, he was inclined to lure defenders into a false sense of security. But, because of his anticipation, they were all left pondering the extent to which appearances can be deceptive.

One of the goals which best epitomised why he was so successful was the one he scored to give the Germans their 3–2 win over England in the World Cup quarter-final in Mexico in 1970. When England centre-half Brian Labone attempted to reach a ball that had been headed back across his goal, Müller, sensing that he was going to miss it, resisted the temptation to challenge him in favour of getting into the space where he felt the ball might drop. Even then he didn't have the easiest of shots because the ball wasn't directly in front of him. However, he was able to twist his thick-set body quickly enough to get a shot on target, and past the England keeper, Peter Bonetti.

Another goal for which he is well remembered was his last at international level, when that uncanny knack of finding space in the box was followed by the quick turn and the close-range shot that brought West Germany their 2–1 win over Holland in the 1974 World Cup final.

During a career spanning fifteen years, his predatory instincts, which he always struggled to articulate, resulted in his scoring 365 goals in 427 matches for Bayern. For West Germany, it was 68 goals in 62 matches, a record that has never been surpassed. His goals-to-game ratio was even better than that of Pele, the scorer of 77 goals in 92 matches for Brazil, and Ferenc Puskas, who got 83 in 84 games for Hungary. More recently, the outstanding scorer in international football has been Gabriel Batistuta, who scored 56 goals in 78 matches for Argentina.

Batistuta and Müller could hardly be more different. If Müller was at the bottom end of the overall-contribution scale, Batistuta, with his tremendous pace, stamina and ball-playing ability, has been at the other. Many managers hold up the Argentinian as the perfect role model for their strikers. Craig Brown says that whenever he hears strikers 'moaning' that the general work demanded of them is detracting from their scoring potential, he tells them, 'Look at Batistuta.'

Brown's insistence that no striker can be a law unto himself also comes across in his negative attitude to such men getting bonuses for scoring. It is not unheard of for the contracts of strikers to include clauses relating to extra payments linked to their scoring records. This was the case with some of Preston's strikers when Brown became manager of the club in April 2002, but Brown has gradually put an end to it. 'It's dangerous,' he said, arguing that though all strikers need to be single-minded about scoring, club bonuses for doing so would lead to the situation Wenger highlighted when discussing strikers being too greedy to score for the good of their teams, and could easily have an adverse effect on team unity.

It is a question of balance, of course, but for the strikers who have the ability to get the most goals and bring their teams the most victories, the right balance is never easy to achieve. While taking into account the ways in which the game has changed, some believe that a number of today's strikers are not single-minded enough about scoring and tend to be too subservient in their relationships with their colleagues. Even Thierry Henry, for all his brilliance, can invoke mixed feelings about his sense of priorities. Gary Pallister, admitted that he has never been able to get his brain around the sight of Henry taking corners. 'I see him doing it week in, week out and I cannot understand it,' he said. 'How can you, as a scorer, be out there taking corners when there might be a great scoring chance to be had in the middle? If you were to ask somebody like Alan Shearer to take a corner, he would probably tell you to get lost.'

One striker who has invited particular criticism about his level of assertiveness in that area is Emile Heskey. And what can one make of the manner in which Southampton striker Kevin Phillips has reinvented himself since his days as the Premiership's top marksman?

Nobody could say that Phillips didn't have a powerful desire to be a scorer at the start of his career, even after Southampton, who had signed him as an apprentice, had decided he was too small and weak physically to make it as a striker and switched him to right-back. 'It was difficult for me to accept,' he said. 'As a kid, I was scoring sixty to seventy goals a season, and I found the right-back role, just defending and giving the ball to the attacking players, quite boring. When I saw the lads up front scoring, I thought, "I want to be doing that." I wanted the limelight.' When Southampton released him, Phillips, at the age of eighteen, drifted into non-league football with the Hertfordshire club Baldock Town, where he was moved back to the striker role and where the experience of playing in a highly physical league, with and against players considerably older and more aggressive than himself, had a 'toughening-up' effect.

The next stage of his development came at Watford, through the coaching and encouragement of their manager, Glenn Roeder. Then, in the summer of 1997, it was on to Sunderland (in the Nationwide League First Division) and a striking partnership with Niall Quinn that was to make him the most prolific scorer in the game. It was the Little and Large show, the 6ft 4in Quinn doing most of the spadework, driving himself towards the long balls or crosses, and the 5ft 5in Phillips – quick, razor sharp and a superb striker of the ball – feeding off him. Phillips recalled, 'I have lost count of the number of goals I scored by latching on to Niall's headed flick-ons. A lot of strikers are happy just to get their heads to a high ball, but Niall was able to sort of hang in mid-air and direct the ball exactly where he wanted to. His headers to me were passes.'

In those days, Phillips was little more than a finisher. But Sunderland were not complaining. In his first season, Phillips broke Brian Clough's post-war scoring record for the club with 35, which included scoring in nine successive home matches – another record. The next season, the 1998/99 campaign, he scored 25, despite being out of action for four months through injury, to help steer Sunderland to promotion. In his first season in the Premiership he was the top league scorer with 35, a total that was also good enough to bring him the distinction of becoming the first Englishman to win the European Golden Boot award.

Since then, though, Phillips has not come anywhere near matching that achievement. In the league, his goal total dropped to fourteen in 2000/01, eleven in 2001/02 and six in 2002/03 – his last Sunderland season, when the team's misery over being relegated was compounded by their losing every one of their last fifteen league matches. 'I was coming off the pitch without having had one chance,' Phillips recalled. 'The team had changed, and I didn't want to be there to be honest, which didn't help.' Perhaps the major problem for him was the decline of Quinn. Troubled by a back problem, the veteran had finally been forced to retire in November 2002 at the age of 36. However, the dearth of goals also stemmed from Phillips's desire to become a better all-round player.

He put it this way: 'It was towards the end of my Sunderland career that I started dropping deeper and got more involved in matches. When I look back on it now, part of me says that perhaps I should not have done that. But although my first three seasons at Sunderland had been fantastic for me, goal-wise, there were many times when I walked off the pitch at the end not completely happy with my game. Even if I had scored two or three goals, I wasn't totally content. I suppose I became spoilt. Goals were no longer enough for me. I wanted everything, to score and also to have an outstanding game in other areas. Proving myself a good all-round player became more important to me when it became clear that I wasn't going to get that many goals anyway in the team I was in. I remember Steve Cotterill [Sunderland's assistant manager in Phillips's last season at the club] telling me, "You've stopped making runs in behind [into the space behind defenders]." He was right, but as I had previously been making those runs for some time without getting the ball, I'd thought, "Why should I keep doing this?" As I was developing other aspects of my game, it was difficult to change.'

Scoring still means a lot to him, if only because of his determination to show that his partnership with Quinn was helpful but not essential to him. As he said to me shortly after his transfer to Southampton during 2003, 'Everyone associates me with Niall. It makes me hungry to show that I can get along without him.' Even so, it was only after Christmas that he truly got back into the scoring habit, and his final league total for the Saints for 2003/04 was twelve.

For all his good work in other aspects of the game, Phillips's recent scoring record will have been viewed with some disdain by a striker as focused as Brian Clough was. Not for nothing did Clough achieve the best post-war goal ratio of any striker in English football, albeit mainly in the old Second Division. His record for Middlesbrough and Sunderland, from 1953 to 1961, was 267 goals in 296 games. At Middlesbrough, his manager, Bob Dennison, once told Clough about a complaint he had received about him from another member of the team. Dennison explained, 'The player says that every time he has the ball close to goal, you shout, "Give it to me," even when he has a good chance of a shot. Why do you do that?'

Clough just shrugged. 'Because I am better at it than he is,' he replied.

'I was king of the castle, king of the castle,' he has said. 'I used to stick it through their bloody legs and say, "Now pick that out."'

Among those whom Clough will surely have recognised as kindred spirits were Malcolm Macdonald and Steve Archibald. They were poles apart as people: Macdonald was gregarious and uninhibited, very much the public showman, while Archibald came across as introverted and uncommunicative. But both men, as knowledgeable and articulate on the art of scoring as any ex-strikers one could find, had similar scoring mentalities. Neither was a shrinking violet in recognising that consistently putting the ball in the net had to be their main priority, or, equally importantly, in pushing for set-ups conducive to their chances of doing this. 'Squeezing the lemon' is how Archibald described it. 'You could say I was a tad demanding,' he said. 'I would think that any striker worth his salt has to be.' It seems difficult to dispute that the single-mindedness with which Archibald and Macdonald pursued this concept, combined with the depth of their thinking about their jobs, was one of the main reasons for their excellent scoring records and, in turn, the success of their teams.

Of all the football figures I have met, Archibald, now living in Spain where he is a football transfer market 'broker' and is also involved in the fields of property acquisition and business development, has struck me as being the closest equivalent to the former England goalkeeping legend Peter Shilton. It was not enough for Shilton to be widely recognised as the number one keeper in the world just through his dedication to training, his off-the-field professional habits and his performances; it was also important to him to look the part, to portray the image one might expect of someone in that lofty position, through the house he lived in, his car and clothes, and the money his clubs paid him. In making managers aware of the importance of having a keeper with his ability, Shilton was nothing if not persuasive. Some of his team-mates felt that he lived in a world of his own, which for the purposes of maintaining his number-one image (and the sense of authority emanating from it) was something else he sought to develop. He once told me, 'I don't do much socialising with team-mates, partly because I feel that the dominating role I like to have in teams would be weakened if people got too close to me. I want to be my own man. The people you work with can see you, get to know you, too much. It just isn't me.'

No player can have had a stronger personality than Shilton. This certainly came in handy in his attempts to persuade the players immediately in front of him that instead of him adapting his approach to the game to suit theirs, it had to be the other way around. He once recalled an England training session during which manager Ron Greenwood organised an exercise involving himself and three other players to give the latter 'third man running' and shooting practice. The three men positioned themselves just outside the penalty area and the object of the exercise was for one player to pass to another, then run forward to receive the final pass from the third player inside the box and have a shot. 'Shots were coming in from between the penalty spot and the edge of the box,' said Shilton, 'and as I was only two or three yards off my line I was having to react to them. I thought, "This isn't right – you're allowing them to dictate to you." So what I did was move further off my line, before the final pass was made, so I was now dictating to them. It could be argued that I ruined the session for the other players, but then I see no reason to apologise for doing my job as a goalkeeper.'

Archibald, seemingly as dogged about the importance of goalscorers to a team as Shilton was about that of goalkeepers, can appreciate where he was coming from. When I first raised the subject of Shilton's desire to build up his image with Archibald some years ago, at a time when his career as a player was drawing to a close at Hibernian, he said, 'I hope you will be careful how you write this – I would hate to give people the wrong impression of me – but I have been similar. While I would never openly describe myself as a star, I do try and live the part in some ways. I was the same even in my early days. Some people might think it's being flash, but it isn't. I honestly feel it had a beneficial psychological effect on me as a player.'

More recently, when we touched on the subject again in an interview for this book, he added, 'When I joined Tottenham [from Aberdeen], I remember the club secretary Peter Day telling me, "The biggest adjustment you will have to make here will not be on the football side, it will be on the financial side. You will have a problem knowing what to do with the extra money you will be earning." It was a good point because I was only a young lad. But earning a lot more money did not affect my hunger for success – it was the opposite. When you come down [to England] as an established striker, you have to act like one. The whole package [the ability and the image] has to be right. The extra money enabled me to maintain my lifestyle and that, among a number of other factors, helped me keep my edge.'

One man at Tottenham who found Archibald's mentality particularly enlightening was John Syer, the club's sports psychologist. 'Steve was wonderful to work with,' Syer said. 'He had an amazing mind.' In one 'creative visualisation' session, Archibald summed up his attitude to scoring by telling Syer that when he had a scoring opportunity he felt like 'a hungry bear suddenly let out of a cage'. Equally telling was his response to Syer's question about what he felt like when he had scored. 'I am the Lord of the Manor,' Archibald told him.

Archibald smiles over the memory. 'He told you about that, did he? All players are important to a team, obviously, but I think that most people would agree that goals decide games and are what everybody wants. So if you are the main scorer at a club, you're liable to be recognised as the main man – it's as simple as that. Rightly or wrongly, that is the way it has always been in football. There's no feeling quite like it, and as a player I was always stimulated by it and wanted to maintain it.

'Obviously, the extent to which you allow this to come through can depend a great deal on the nature of your club. For example, Aberdeen are a small, tightly knit club, which was reflected by the attitudes and mentalities of the players I worked with there. It was like being in a close family. It was different at clubs like Tottenham and Barcelona. Having so-called 'stars' – players with egos, if you want to put it that way – was part of their culture. When you go home, you are a different person, but when you have that "main man" image you have to take it with you into the dressing room and on to the field, in both training and matches. You are The Man, and everybody expects you to be The Man. You have to deliver.'

Lord of the Manor? Archibald, an exceptionally ambitious person, will have had no qualms about taking on that guise (and all the pressure that goes with it) right from the very start of his career in Scotland, when he combined an apprenticeship as a Rolls-Royce motor mechanic with playing as a part-time professional for Clyde. Craig Brown was Clyde's manager then, and Archibald was able to develop his noted overall ability there by filling every position for the club, including that of goalkeeper. Such was his ability to read the game that, in those days, he felt his best position was that of sweeper. It was at Aberdeen, where he worked under Billy McNeill and then Alex Ferguson and progressed from midfield to a front-line role, that the notion of becoming one of Britain's most respected post-war scorers started to take root. As Ferguson, a former centre-forward, was cast in the same aggressive mould as Archibald, it wasn't unusual for the two men to be in conflict. In fact, they had so many arguments in Fergie's Pittodrie office that the manager named the chair his striker sat in 'Archibald's Chair'. It says much about Ferguson's respect for Archibald, however, that the Old Trafford supremo has since gone on record describing him as one of his all-time favourite players.

The more Archibald progressed up the soccer ladder, the more strong-willed and assertive he seemed to become. 'It was due to the experience I had gained, the knowledge that what I had been doing had worked,' he explained. One wonders what might have happened to him had this not been the case at Barcelona. He was virtually unknown in Spain when Terry Venables brought him to the club. In those days, clubs in that country were allowed to sign only two foreign players, and Archibald's attempts to gain credibility among his highly skilled fellow players and the ultra-critical Nou Camp fans were not helped by the fact that the star he effectively replaced was Diego Maradona. 'You have to give them [team mates] the confidence to think they can work with you,' Archibald said. 'Quite apart from showing them that you are on the same wavelength in technical ability, it's also a question of proving that you have the necessary mental strength.' In that respect, Archibald 'threw down the gauntlet' on his very first day of training at the club. Having been given Maradona's old locker, he promptly asked a club official to replace the Argentinian's name on it with his.

Those who felt that Archibald was 'difficult' might well argue that Tottenham's captain when he joined the club, Steve Perryman, had a lot to answer for. According to Archibald, it was Perryman who did the most to cause him to look upon himself as a 'natural' goalscorer, as opposed to a forward. He explained, 'Soon after I joined Spurs, Steve came up to me and said, "I'm convinced that we are going to be successful now we have signed a natural goalscorer like you." Nobody had ever described me in that way before. I knew I could score goals, obviously, but I had never thought of myself as a "natural scorer". At Aberdeen I didn't really have the experience to be able to define what I was as a footballer, and maybe having someone I respected doing it was what I was looking for at that time. I trusted Steve's judgement, and that comment was a major turning point for me.'

A turning point that inevitably led Archibald to become more sensitive than ever about strikers getting the right service. For example, during our conversation, I struck a chord with him by mentioning the advice Southampton's James Beattie had been given once by his then club manager Gordon Strachan. In addition to encouraging Beattie to reprimand any team-mate who had not given him the type of pass or cross he needed to score, Strachan told him, 'Don't wait until half-time or after the game to do it. Do it at the time.' This was not something Archibald needed to be told, and when he did deem it necessary to express his displeasure with a colleague over not getting the ball at the right time or in the right way, he admitted that he did not believe in diplomacy. 'You have to adopt an aggressive or angry manner in these situations – that's what I would tell any striker. A lot of times, this really is the most effective way of getting the message across.'

Archibald recognises that he was fortunate to operate with men as skilful on the ball as Strachan (at Aberdeen), Ossie Ardiles and Glenn Hoddle (Tottenham) and Bernt Schuster (Barcelona). Nonetheless, even with these figures, Archibald says that he occasionally felt the need to impose himself. 'Sometimes, the ability that these sort of players have can create problems for a front man because when they play the ball to you they often want it back; they can play a ball to you in a way in which they are basically only lending it to you. I feel that a number of strikers in that situation do not truly understand what is happening and how it might be detracting from their potential as scorers. When they're repeatedly being used as a "wall" they will get a certain amount of satisfaction out of not losing possession etc. But it seems to me that being forced into this role can become so much of a habit that, while they might have a vague feeling that something isn't quite right, they struggle to really pinpoint the problem.

'All strikers like that should watch Ronaldo, especially when he is playing with David Beckham [for Real Madrid]. If you watch his matches, you will notice that he doesn't come deep to link the play. He realises that, because of his past injury problems, he can no longer cope with opponents hacking at his legs from behind, so when Beckham is on the ball you will see him right on the shoulder of the defender, looking for a pass into the space behind him. He will dictate where he wants the ball to go just through his body language and his positioning. Others have to do it differently, and I'm all in favour of it. When it comes to getting the right service, you have to demand certain things and you cannot be afraid to have showdowns with people.'

For Archibald, this also applied to the question of his involvement in his teams' defensive work. Once described by his highly respected former Hibernian manager Alex Miller as the best attacking 'technician' he had ever worked with, Archibald was no slouch in broadening his outlook and helping his teams in other aspects of the game. He was one of the most complete strikers of his generation and, as indicated by the versatility he showed at Clyde, did not look out of place in most areas of the field. At the same time, he was always conscious of the need to know where to draw the line.

'I understood that I couldn't concentrate just on scoring,' he said. 'If a manager told me to drop back to the halfway line when we lost the ball, or shuttle across to stop the full-back breaking forward with it, I wasn't against that in principle. But if I thought that an instruction was detrimental to my ability to score, then I would have to discuss it with him.'

Even his arguments with Alex Ferguson (which he says helped maintain his aggression on the pitch) were mild in comparison with one clash with his Tottenham boss, Keith Burkinshaw. The relationship between Burkinshaw and Archibald, two of the proudest and most stubborn figures one could find in the game, was always difficult. The most famous explosion point arose from an incident in a match against Coventry during the 1983/84 season when Archibald signalled to the bench that he had sustained an injury and needed to be substituted. Burkinshaw, who felt that Archibald had made too much of the injury, was quoted in the media accusing him of 'cheating', which prompted Archibald to refuse to talk to him. The situation continued even after the manager had made a private apology to him, because of Archibald's insistence that it had to be a public one. This was never forthcoming, but it was typical of Archibald that he scored his highest number of goals for Spurs that season (33) and helped them win the Uefa Cup.

Another row between Burkinshaw and Archibald took place during a training match because of Burkinshaw's persistent attempts to instruct the striker to operate as a defensive marker when Spurs were facing free-kicks and corners. 'I have never been in such a confrontational situation in my life,' Archibald recalled. 'Whenever we conceded a free-kick or corner I had to come back to mark someone, while Crooksey [Garth Crooks, his striking partner] was left up the field. I didn't mind that, but after doing it time after time I thought Crooksey should share the job. That's what all strikers do. Burkinshaw called me back again when we had to face another corner, and as I was walking towards him I said, "Hang on a minute, why can't Crooksey come back this time?" Burkinshaw said, "No, you come back. You are better marking at corners than he is." True, I was taller than him, but I felt he could jump as high as I could; I couldn't see how having him challenging for a ball in the air instead of me was going to cause a problem. Burkinshaw, though, would not have any of it, so I said, "No, I'm not going to do it," and walked back to the middle of the field. The atmosphere was unbelievable. But finally, Crooksey said, "I'll go back," and that was it.'

Does Archibald have any regrets about digging his heels in so firmly?

'Well, it was unfortunate that it came to that, but I couldn't have backed down because had I done so, what would the other players have been thinking about me? You have to take into account the numerous little psychological factors involved in the game. Had I backed down, they would have taken the view that I had bottled it. This would surely have had an adverse effect on what I was asking of them on the Saturday.'

Malcolm Macdonald could easily have anticipated how Burkinshaw's football philosophy would affect his relationship with Archibald because Supermac also had big rows with the manager, for the same reason, when the pair were at Newcastle United. 'Keith [then Newcastle's coach] was forever on to me about helping out the defence,' Macdonald has told me. 'He wanted me to chase back and harass opponents when we lost the ball, things like that. But I couldn't see the point. As a striker, I relied on sudden, explosive bursts and felt I would quickly get knackered if I couldn't take the

A left-footed snap-shot from the master finisher, Jimmy Greaves

Diego Maradona weaves another magic spell and cuts through the English back line once more during that epic match in the 1986 World Cup quarter-finals

Alan Shearer has been English football's most prolific marksman over the past decade

Brazilian Ronaldo's electrifying speed and upper body strength are guaranteed to cause problems for even the tightest of defensive formations

A trademark Michael Owen finish, tucked away beyond the keeper's reach

For such a short man, Paul Scholes' aerial ability is legendary. His goal-scoring record goes to prove what can be achieved from a world-class midfield operator

Thierry Henry's wonderful athleticism has enabled him – and his club – to become the most potent attacking force in the Premiership

Ruud van Nistelrooy's all-round scoring prowess and insatiable appetite for goals have catapulted him into the very top bracket of world-class poachers

necessary recovery time. We used to have the most incredible rows over this.'

At Arsenal, Macdonald also crossed swords with coach Don Howe, especially during a training session during which he was called upon to go into wide positions to create scoring space for a team-mate bursting through from deep positions. Macdonald recalled, 'I told Don, "Why do you want me out here, when I can score goals, and him in there, when he can't score? That cannot be right." He told me I was complicating things, but to me, I was simplifying them. I said, "Look, what ball am I going to knock in? The kind of ball I like to receive will be no good to him, because he won't know what the hell to do with it, whereas if he's out there he can knock any ball he likes to me and I will get on the end of it." I wouldn't let it go – I couldn't.'

Macdonald suggested that the belligerence with which he rejected appeals to address himself to other aspects of the game was something of a defence mechanism. Referring to the shortage of strings to his bow outside his scoring ability, he said, 'I couldn't "play". Coaches found me difficult to handle because I always had this protective barrier up. "Don't ask me to do that, I don't want to do it," I would say. What I was really saying was that I couldn't do it because I wasn't good enough.' This, he added, helps explain his apparent scoring bravado. 'I was a great believer in publicly projecting my strengths. In media interviews before a match, I would be quite happy to be quoted as saying that I would score. People used to say, "You bighead – I don't know how you have the front to do it." But I knew what I was doing. You know, while the attitude of coaches like Burkinshaw and Howe was that I should try to improve my weak points, mine was, "Blow your weaknesses – build up your strengths to the point where they could hide a million bloody weaknesses."'

As a consequence, Macdonald was a striker for whom the words 'selfish' and 'greedy' could have been invented. This, for example, is what he once told me about his attitude to shooting: 'I shot from anywhere and everywhere. Players used to throw their arms up and say, "I don't believe it. What are you doing?" I'd say sorry, but I wasn't sorry at all. I knew what I was doing. If you don't buy a ticket, you can't win the Lottery, can you? Also, I had to find out whether I could score from certain positions. At Luton, I even used to shoot from corners – honestly I did. I'd take them from the right, with my left foot, and if I saw the keeper slightly off his line I'd try to curl the ball into the net. Usually the ball would sail over the bar or go straight over to the other side of the field for a throw-in. The other players would say to Jimmy Andrews [Luton's coach], "Get him off corners, Jimmy. He's useless." They didn't appreciate I was trying to score from them. They just thought I was a bad corner-taker. The more goals I scored, the more single-minded – all right, arrogant – I became. I must have been unbearable to live with at times.'

This was also reflected by his reaction to the principle of strikers 'hunting' in pairs. 'The way I looked at it was that strikers play in pairs; they do not hunt in pairs. When it came to strikers sharing the scoring responsibility, I think I was probably too selfish to hunt with anybody.' His most democratic partnership was the one with Frank Stapleton at Arsenal in the late 1970s, but at the start of it, when Stapleton was eighteen and Macdonald 26, Supermac recalled, 'I dominated him. Some of the best partnerships are those in which one striker does all or most of the spadework and the other puts the ball in the net. In those days, however, I took advantage of my seniority by making him run about all over the place. All I did was look to get on the end of the final ball and stick it into the net. I remember him saying to me, "Why is it that I keep making all your goals and you never make me any?" I told him that I had been expected to do what he did when I was his age. As it happened, the big difference between Frank and myself was that I didn't do it, but of course I didn't tell Frank that.'

Of the clubs Macdonald played for, Newcastle United seemed to provide the most appropriate home for him. Newcastle have a great tradition for having prolific goalscorers, especially top-scoring centre-forwards. At no club in Britain are these number 9s fêted by the fans more than they are at St James's Park. Even Macdonald tends to get somewhat starry-eyed when recalling the names of some of those who wore that jersey before him. He has said that one of his most influential experiences at Newcastle came at the very start of his career there when he met Jackie Milburn, the legendary Newcastle and England centre-forward of the 1940s and 1950s who was then working in the city as a football journalist. Macdonald's fondest memory of the late Milburn concerns the way in which the old star put his mind at rest over what was expected of him at a club of Newcastle's stature. Macdonald, having never been in the top flight before, asked, 'What do I need to do to win over the fans?' Milburn replied, simply, 'Just score goals. Do that, and the fans will love you.'

Today, another centre-forward in the traditional British mould has established a similar love affair with the Geordie public. He can seem to get quite tetchy when you raise the subject of Supermac with him – the result of his sensitivity over one or two of Macdonald's criticisms of his performances in the media, and perhaps Macdonald's apparent brashness. When I interviewed him, and suggested that one of his comments about scoring ('You must never be afraid to miss') was virtually a carbon copy of what Macdonald had once written in a book, he muttered, 'I certainly didn't get it from him.' However, Macdonald would be the first to concede that in his way this striker presents arguably the best example of all a goalscorer can achieve with the right mentality.

The name is Shearer.

CHAPTER SIX
STRENGTH IN ADVERSITY

'For a striker, there are so many factors
that can stop you doing what you want
to do. It is how you react to them –
that's the most important thing.'

ALAN SHEARER

The footballers who tend to command the greatest respect are those who keep reminding us of the maxim 'When the going gets tough, the tough get going'. Strength in adversity is a major success factor in all football-playing countries, but it has long been associated mainly with British teams, and more specifically with British players; and it is often the men at the front end of those teams who have done the most to provide the lead. These strikers have usually been tall, powerfully built centre-forwards with styles of play that have mirrored the renowned physical power and competitiveness of British football. Quite apart from their goals, they have represented the heart and soul of their teams.

Among the most famous members of the breed is Nat Lofthouse, the Bolton and England centre-forward of the 1950s. To this day, Lofthouse is still known as the 'Lion of Vienna', the nickname he was given for his stirring two-goal performance during England's 3–2 win over Austria in May 1952. The match was billed as the 'unofficial championship of Europe', and also as a clash between the 'new' and 'old' ways of playing the game. England seemed stuck in a tactical time-warp, as Hungary were to emphasise the following year with their 6–3 hiding of England at Wembley. But on this occasion, with Lofthouse leading England's forward line, it didn't matter. His winning goal eight minutes from the end encapsulated all that foreign teams have always admired about their British counterparts. Having received a pass from Tom Finney, Lofthouse showed tremendous will-power as he ran 45 yards with the ball with a pack of defenders snapping at his heels. As he produced his decisive shot, he was knocked unconscious in a collision with the Austrian keeper, and was thus probably the only person in the stadium who did not see the ball roll over the line. Lofthouse was carried off but, though still dazed, insisted on returning to the action for the last five minutes. Not content to just try and help England preserve their lead, he struck a shot against a post in the closing moments.

In recent years, no striker has highlighted this bulldog spirit as impressively and in as many different ways as Alan Shearer – the striker who can teach us the most about the secrets of being an outstanding scorer in English football. He is the highest Premiership scorer in the league's history; he became the youngest player ever to score a hat-trick at the top level in England (against Arsenal on his full league debut for Southampton at the age of seventeen in April 1988); he was the first player to reach the 100-goal and 200-goal milestones in the Premiership; with Newcastle's Andy Cole, he holds the record for the highest number of Premiership goals in one season (34 for Blackburn in 1994/95), not to mention the record for the highest number of goals in one game (five for Newcastle against Chelsea in 1999); and in the 1995/96 campaign, when his Blackburn team were at their lowest ebb, he became the first player to score 30 goals or more in the top flight in three successive seasons. By the end of the 2003/04 season, his overall Premiership total, including penalties, was 243 in 381 matches; if one includes all his senior club matches at the top level, for Southampton as well as for Blackburn and Newcastle, the figure is 346 goals in 650 games. For England, he got 30 in 63 matches. What makes all this particularly impressive is that Shearer has never been in an outstanding club team, and is not the most gifted of players. Little wonder that most managers and coaches single him out as the ultimate striker role model.

Players can be confronted by many psychological, physical and technical barriers throughout their careers. 'You expect that,' Shearer said. 'For a striker, there are so many factors that can stop you doing what you want to do. It is how you react to them – that's the most important thing.'

In all his time working with Alan Smith at Leeds, Eddie Gray's fondest memory of the striker was his reaction to the threat to his first-team place at the start of the 2000/01 season. Gray, then assistant manager, said, 'With Mark Viduka having joined the club from Celtic, and Michael Bridges emerging as our top scorer the previous season, it looked as if Alan would struggle to get a place in our starting line-up. David O'Leary [then the Leeds manager] asked me to have a word with Alan about this, and as I was doing so, on the pitch before a friendly match at Huddersfield, David came on to the field to join us. Alan, with no trace of anger or resentment, told him, "I think I am a better player than Viduka and Bridges put together, and I am going to prove it to you." People have knocked Alan because of his hot-headedness and his poor disciplinary record, but that incident told another story about him. Instead of throwing his dummy out of the pram, as a lot of highly acclaimed young strikers might have done, Alan looked upon the situation as a challenge that could bring the best out of him.' That season, Smith, in partnership with Viduka, led Leeds to the European Champions League semi-final.

Henrik Larsson was confronted with a challenge of a different and more agonising kind in October 1999, when his achievement in clinching the Celtic record for getting 50 league goals for the club in the shortest period was quickly followed by his fracturing both his tibia and fibula. The following season, Larsson was the top scorer in Europe.

Ruud van Nistelrooy showed similar strength of character by fighting back from his cruciate ligament injury prior to his move to Manchester United. When asked once to pinpoint the secrets of his success, van Nistelrooy said, 'I feel you are always striving to prove a point to people, a point to yourself in a way, that you can score goals on a consistent basis. I have a good awareness and a pretty good turn of speed, but it's the hunger and determination that sets you apart from other players. When I came to England, I had a pretty good record in Holland, but after the knee injury I think people wondered whether I would be the same player. I have always had tremendous faith in my ability and I have always had supportive people around me. And if you want something enough, no matter how hard you have to work, if you are prepared to give everything, you can climb mountains.'

Shearer, who has also overcome serious injuries, has thrived on all manner of battles against the odds. Being between a rock and a hard place has never bothered him. In fact, it's when he's in that situation that he has often been at his best. Hence the willingness of his teams to put their trust in him, as Blackburn did when they made him the focal point of their side and he responded by leading them to the Premiership title, at the expense of more talented teams, in 1995.

One of the many ways in which Shearer's exemplary temperament has been illustrated is through his record of scoring on his debuts for all his teams. He even did it for England against France at Wembley in February 1992, despite the pressure on him as a result of the exclusion of Gary Lineker from the starting line-up.

At a time when England were struggling to cause any major problems for the French defence, it was Shearer who broke the deadlock. Then Lineker came on to replace David Hirst, and it was Shearer who set him up for the second England goal in a 2–0 win. Perhaps his biggest scoring challenge came at Euro 96. Before the start of the tournament, his run of twelve matches without an England goal – a disappointing 21-month spell during which he had often operated up front virtually on his own and been troubled by a groin injury – inevitably prompted the widespread view that he should be dropped. Trust Shearer to respond to that by emerging as the competition's top scorer, with five goals, to help propel England to the semi-final stage.

This characteristic in Shearer has been prevalent since the very start of his career, and it needed to be. He scored plenty of goals as a schoolboy, but Newcastle, his home-city club, allowed him to slip out of their net because he lacked the flair of others available to them. Some felt that Shearer was too 'one-paced', slightly built and limited in his work on the ball to establish an outstanding career. But Shearer did not let that get to him. He told me, 'Providing they are not personal, the opinions of other people [about his shortcomings as a footballer] do not bother me. I have always had belief in myself and gone my way rather than anyone else's. If it goes wrong, then I know I only have myself to blame. I like it that way.'

No less confident about Shearer's ability to reach the top was Jack Hixon, the scout who recommended Shearer to Southampton when the player was fourteen. 'What attracted me to Alan,' Hixon recalled, 'was that he had a good football brain and what I would call the three essential fundamentals: attitude, application, character. He struck me as being a lad who would always make the most of what he had got. When I first saw him, I was struck by his positive, aggressive running and his "bottle". To be successful as a striker, you have to be prepared to go into positions where you know you are going to get hurt, and he stood out like a beacon in that way. He just came across as a lad with remarkable strength of character and maturity, and in my experience, if you have these things, you are two thirds of the way there.'

Even so, Southampton, having signed Shearer as a schoolboy, took their time in deciding whether or not to sign him as a trainee professional. The club's youth development officer at that time, Bob Higgins, has been quoted as saying that a few months before Shearer was due to leave school at sixteen he felt the player still 'had a little bit more to do' to convince him he was worth taking on. This, of course, gave Shearer – who was getting somewhat 'edgy' about the situation, according to Hixon – the perfect opportunity to show his mental toughness again. Higgins, in order to make a final assessment of Southampton's schoolboy players and triallists, arranged for them to be put through their paces together at a teacher-training centre in Hampshire during the 1986 Easter period. The training sessions were followed by a full-scale final trial match in which Shearer outshone everybody else by scoring five goals. As the fifth one went in, Shearer, understandably high on the adrenalin of clearing what he perceived to be the last obstacle to a Southampton apprenticeship, looked across at Higgins and showed him the five fingers of his hand.

At this point, a member of the Southampton coaching staff who had been watching the match alongside Hixon remarked, 'We will be taking Alan.'

'Thought so,' Hixon replied, wryly.

Having got his foot in the door at Southampton, Shearer did not find himself short of other admirers. Jimmy Case, the former Liverpool and England midfielder who was Southampton's captain as Shearer progressed through the ranks there, recalled, 'The first description that came into my mind when I saw Alan was "power player". From an early age I thought he showed tremendous power in holding off defenders, getting past them, and I was also impressed by his shooting power. I would stay behind after training to help Dennis Rofe [the Southampton coach] in giving players any extra work they or the club felt was necessary, and Alan was one of the lads I came into contact with the most. His appetite for learning his trade was remarkable. You knew that he was going to squeeze the absolute maximum out of himself. Of all the youngsters at the club when I was there, he was the top man as far as I was concerned. In fact, I used to say to him, "If ever I become a manager, I am going to come and get you."'

Shearer's biggest flaw then concerned his first touch. Chris Nicholl, Southampton's manager for four of Shearer's five seasons there as a full-time professional, was once quoted as saying that initially the centre-forward 'couldn't trap a bag of cement'. However, while most people felt that Shearer was at his best when he was facing the opposing goal and the ball was played in front of him, this did not stop Nicholl (and Shearer) striving for the improvement in his ball skills that would enable him to add another dimension to his game. 'I saw no reason why he could not operate as a target man [as a striker who could receive the ball to his feet, with his back to the goal],' Nicholl said, 'for the simple reason that, like strikers such as Kenny Dalglish and Mark Hughes, he did have a big backside and big, powerful thighs. The first priority for a target man is to be able to "protect" the ball, and the way Alan was built made him ideal for this as far as I was concerned. Dalglish's build was one of the reasons why I found him the most difficult player to mark when I was playing [as a centre-half]. It was the way he used his backside and hips to keep you away from the ball. In fact, not only did he stop you from getting to the ball, often you couldn't even see it. You thought you might be able to get a touch, but then bang, his hips and leg would come across and would be shoved into you. After a match against Dalglish, my thighs would be covered in bruises. Physically, Alan had the same things going for him, and we felt this was a great foundation for us to work on. In training, we would keep hitting the ball to him and it would keep breaking away from him. We had him out for extra practice on this almost every day; I lost count of the number of hours I spent just throwing balls at him from every angle. But he would never give up. He was determined to learn his trade.'

During his Southampton career, Shearer scored ten goals in eleven England under-21 matches and two in three senior international matches. Strange as it might seem, though, his goal total from his 118 Southampton league appearances was just 23. It was only in his last season there, when Ian Branfoot had succeeded Nicholl as manager, that he emerged as the club's leading scorer. Even then, his record of thirteen goals in 41 matches, while more than reasonable in the light of his team's struggle against relegation, was hardly earth-shattering. One explanation is that, despite Shearer's remarkable hat-trick against Arsenal in his first full league match, Nicholl, in common with many other managers with exciting young players, had been sensitive about exposing him to the pressures of regular first-team football too early. He preferred to make Shearer's development a gradual process.

Under Nicholl, Southampton usually operated with only one recognised central striker. Their most effective combination turned out to be Shearer at centre-forward with the exceptionally quick and mobile Rod Wallace on the right and the extravagantly gifted Matthew Le Tissier on the left. Shearer was very much the focal point for attacks, with the two others feeding off him. It did seem to make sense because, although being virtually the workhorse detracted from Shearer's own scoring ability, his finishing could be somewhat erratic, anyway. Wallace and Le Tissier, both older and more experienced than he was, were more clinical.

But there was no doubt that Shearer's attitude was a key element in the team. Southampton's full-back, Jason Dodd, recalled, 'It was great for me to have someone like him at centre-forward because if I was in trouble at the back I could just bang the ball forward and he would give a hundred per cent in trying to make something of it. It didn't need to be a good ball to him, because you could be sure he would turn it into a half decent one if only by putting enough pressure on defenders to force them to concede a throw-in or corner. He would work his socks off for the team, even if he wasn't playing well. So although he wasn't recognised as the top dog in scoring – Matt and Rod were – he had every bit as much respect from the rest of the lads as they did.'

Jimmy Case, reflecting on the new lease of life he experienced as a Southampton player in his thirties, said, 'I had been spoilt by playing behind Kenny Dalglish at Liverpool. In addition to Kenny's ability on the ball, his vision was amazing. Whenever he got the ball, he seemed to know where everybody was. I lost count of the number of times at Liverpool that I would go on a forward run after giving him the ball and then get it back from him in a position in which I didn't think he had seen me. Alan didn't have that, but he was great for me in other ways. He was what you would call a very straightforward type of striker, so that in itself made him an easy person to play with because you could read him. The runs he made [to receive the ball] were great. At that stage in my career, the last thing I wanted was to have nothing on when I was in possession and have to hold the ball and fight people off before making a pass, because that's more tiring than anything. But Alan was always moving for you. The point is that he would invite me to play the pass which was easy for me; he would not take up a position which would have needed a Pele or Maradona to find him. Also, once you played the ball in front of him, you knew that even if it was only a 50/50 ball for him, the first thing in his mind would be to end up with a shooting chance from it.'

Among others who were to capitalise on this ability was the late Ray Harford, who first came into contact with Shearer when he combined his duties as Wimbledon manager with those of being the head coach of the England under-21 team for the Toulon International Tournament in France in the summer of 1991. Harford, no more than an average Football League centre-half during his own playing career with Charlton, Exeter, Lincoln, Mansfield, Port Vale and Colchester, was inevitably a great believer in teams getting the ball into the opposing danger area as quickly as possible, as opposed to playing what he was fond of describing as 'pretty' football. With a centre-forward like Shearer, whom he looked upon as a kindred spirit in terms of the striker's pragmatic 'working-class' approach to the game, Harford had the perfect excuse to implement his philosophy in the England under-21 set-up.

Harford knew exactly how to fully exploit Shearer's ability and much of his work on the training field was devoted to this. One aspect of it concerned the confusion between the England under-21 central defender Carl Tiler and Shearer in the opening match, when the former came forward with the ball and the latter came towards him with the aim of suddenly spinning off the man marking him to take the ball behind him. Tiler, though, played the ball to his feet, and Shearer, taken by surprise, was easily dispossessed; then, when Shearer wanted the ball to his feet, Tiler played it long for him.

In these situations, the onus is usually on the striker to give the man in possession a clear indication of the sort of pass he wants. Some strikers do it with subtle hand signals. Jimmy Case recalled that when he played with Rod Wallace, Wallace would do it with his eyes. 'If they were screwed up, it meant that he didn't think there was anything on for him and I should just knock the ball to his feet; if he opened them wide, he just went whoosh. All I had to do was play the ball in behind the defence and he was gone.' In Shearer's case, Harford told him that if he wanted the latter he should shout 'Charlie'. 'I got the idea from Dave Sexton [the former Chelsea and Manchester United manager, and England coach],' Harford told me. 'The only difference was that the strikers he worked with had to use the word "Fiver". He always referred to that sort of pass to a striker as the "Fiver ball", because if the player scored from it he would have to give him a fiver. It's a good thing Dave didn't work with Alan. Alan scored stacks of goals like that.'

In that Toulon tournament, Shearer, appointed England captain by Harford, was the top scorer with seven goals in four matches. These included the only goal in the semi-final against Russia and in the final against France. Harford described him as the English version of the outstanding West German centre-forward Karl-Heinz Rummenigge. 'I fell in love with him,' Harford recalled. 'Absolutely fell in love with him.'

By that stage Southampton and Nicholl had parted company, and Harford was being widely tipped to take over from him. That did not materialise, but before Harford and Shearer did work together again, at Blackburn, Shearer cannot have been disappointed at the way his development was maintained by his new Southampton boss, Ian Branfoot, even though Southampton continued to struggle in the lower half of the table. Branfoot himself became arguably the most unpopular manager in their history among the fans. So much so that a Southampton fanzine even went to the outrageous step of a front-page headline portraying the message that they wished he was dead. Apart from Southampton's results, such hostility also had its roots in the fact that Branfoot didn't have the personality and charisma of his predecessors, and the style of play of his team seemed to emphasise this.

But as that style meant Southampton repeatedly 'hitting' Shearer early and playing lots of 'channel' balls (passes through the gaps between central defenders and full-backs), it suited the centre-forward perfectly. So, too, did the fact that the sale of Rod Wallace to Leeds United was followed by Branfoot giving him a proper central striking partner (initially Paul Rideout, then Iain Dowie). As Shearer said at the time, 'It used to be a case of getting the ball out to Rod or Matt, but now Paul Rideout and I will have a bigger role. While I don't dislike being the target man, having another striker to share the responsibility is bound to help me. I have always said that it suited me playing alongside a central striker, and I do like the direct style of play that the boss is favouring.' Jason Dodd recalled, 'We did a lot of channel-ball practice in training. It wasn't a question of just hitting the ball forward in behind opposing defenders; we were given specific areas to aim for. When you say "You have to get the ball in the area between the right or left touchline and the edge of the eighteen-yard box" it sounds simple, doesn't it? But there is an art to it. If you play too far to one side, then it's liable to run through to the goalkeeper; if you play it too far to the other side, it will run out of play. You also need to play the ball early enough to give the player for whom it is intended a reasonable chance of gaining possession without being caught offside. I thought we did it as well as anyone when Branfoot was the manager. It definitely worked well for Alan.'

Indeed, Shearer's league goal total of thirteen that season was misleading because he had enough chances to have achieved a much higher figure. Branfoot has said, 'He had lots and lots of chances that he failed to put away, so many that instead of finishing sixteenth in the table we should have been in the top six. I don't think any of us could work it out. In the end we just put it down to Alan's inexperience. I was convinced he would just get better and better. He absorbed things very quickly. With some players, you might have to tell them something two or three times before it sticks, but with Alan you only had to tell him once. His general approach to the game was exemplary.

'When I think of my time working with Alan Shearer, the one incident that immediately springs to mind concerns a match in which the other team had the ball deep in their half, and the determination Alan showed in trying to stop them threatening our defence. He made a run from the middle to the right flank to stop their full-back taking the ball forward; and when the full-back played it across to the other flank, Alan burst across to that side as well and chased him almost to the halfway line. When you put that together with his goals – well, despite the chances he missed in the season I worked with him, we all came away thinking, "Yeah, he's smashing. He's got everything. He can't go wrong."'

Shearer had good cause to feel the same way in the 1992 close season when Blackburn Rovers, rolling in money as a result of Jack Walker's lavish patronage of the club, bought him for a then British record transfer fee of £3.5 million. Many accused him of being too money-conscious; surely, they argued, it would have made more sense for him professionally to hold out for a move to Manchester United (who wanted him but were not prepared to pay the transfer fee and wages Blackburn were willing to fork out). Against that, of course, was the challenge Blackburn, as Premiership newcomers, presented for Shearer; and, of course, the fact that Harford was at Blackburn by this time, having formed a managerial partnership there with the great Kenny Dalglish.

Southampton badly missed Shearer, as did Branfoot, who was

sacked two seasons later. Branfoot, stressing that he had been powerless to stop the transfer, said, 'You have to be a manager to fully appreciate the feeling that goes through the dressing room when a great striker has left a club. If I could have paid Shearer four times what the other players were getting – which I couldn't – I don't think it would have bothered them too much. If anything, I think they would have been more bothered about Matthew Le Tissier [probably the most popular player in the club's history among the fans] getting four times more than them.'

The point was emphasised by what Shearer's colleagues at Blackburn thought about him. Harford, who spent five years at Blackburn, once said that his relationship with Shearer during the club's rise to the championship helped make it 'the football adventure of my life'. If anything, Harford, who used to argue that managers or coaches who were once central defenders can often teach centre-forwards more than ex-number 9s can, probably helped Shearer push himself further than even Dalglish did.

In common with a lot of other football geniuses, Dalglish, unlike Harford, was not a particularly good coach in the sense of organising training sessions and team tactics to bring the best out of lesser players. Mike Newell, one of Shearer's striking partners at Blackburn, commented, 'Kenny just wanted to pick his team and let them get on with it. Obviously, he would give advice – he was very astute – but he tended to focus on you as an individual, on your individual ability, whereas Ray dealt with the collective side of things more.' This is where Dalglish and Harford, two men from opposite ends of the football tracks, complemented each other perfectly. They got on well together, both professionally and socially.

Nonetheless, their different ideas on how the game should be played did occasionally bring them into conflict. To Dalglish, Harford's approach at Blackburn was too disciplined and regimented and did not allow players enough scope to express their individuality; to Harford, Dalglish was inclined to lose sight of the fact that precious few players were capable of the skills he and his team-mates at Liverpool had been able to produce, and that attempts to get Blackburn to adhere to exactly the same principles would be tantamount to the team leaving too much to chance. The two men would often have long debates on the subject, but neither would give way. In terms of the basic principles of their arguments, they just agreed to disagree.

As Blackburn were no Liverpool, Harford took the team down the same sort of path Shearer had trodden with Branfoot at Southampton. Like Everton when they won the title in 1985 and 1987, Blackburn were very much a no-frills 4–4–2 team. Shearer himself conceded, 'We were not the most skilful team in the world. But we had a system in which everybody knew his job and was good at it. What we lacked in individual flair we made up for in our work-rate, organisation and commitment.'

Dalglish's view of all this was summed up at the start of the 1994/95 season when he remarked to Harford that he felt Blackburn were too predictable. 'Kenny told me that he was bored with the way the team were playing,' Harford said. 'I said, "I'm bored with it too, Kenny, but if we try to change it now we are liable to fall apart."' To his credit, Dalglish allowed Harford to have his way – and that season, of course, Blackburn went on to win the championship for the first time in 81 years.

As far as Harford's work with Shearer was concerned, one Dalglish criticism concerned Harford's insistence that when the striker invited a pass to his feet, a ball delivered to him from the right should be directed to his right foot and one played to him from the left would need to be directed to his left. Harford felt that Shearer could look a limited player in these situations ('He doesn't really have any tricks to beat you,' he explained). He felt that his passing 'rule' would help offset this. Through his specialist knowledge of the marking habits of defenders, he reasoned that it would usually mean Shearer getting the ball on the side that the opponent breathing down his neck had left 'open'. For his part, Dalglish suggested that in going into such fine detail about the service to Shearer, Harford might have been underestimating the striker's ability and overestimating that of the men who were playing against him. The chances Shearer created suggested otherwise.

Harford also felt that the players then at his disposal were better equipped to hit the opposition on the break than to force the play themselves, and who better than Shearer to make it work for them? He did not have the explosive pace of a Thierry Henry or Michael Owen – Harford viewed him as a strong footballer rather than a particularly quick one – but his intelligence in knowing when and how to break free of defenders, and his determination and physical power in holding them off, made him the most difficult of strikers to stop. Hence Harford's insistence on repeatedly getting Shearer, and the team, 'turned around'. In practice matches, Shearer, on receiving a clearance from his defence, was not allowed to play the ball back. 'He had to turn with it and go forward,' Harford said. 'So the only way you could get a return pass from him would be to move forward into a position alongside him or beyond him. That helped Alan, because having team-mates bursting through, as well as himself, unsettled opposing central defenders.'

Another aspect of Harford's bid to exploit Shearer's ability was Blackburn's work on crosses. Shearer himself saw no reason why, when Blackburn were developing an attack down the flank, one of the wide players should not attempt to 'hit' him with the ball once they got within 30 yards of the goal. Given that Shearer was at his best when facing the goal, Harford insisted on crosses being made from what he described as the 'magic square': the space either side of the eighteen-yard box. 'Give him the right ball from that area and you could almost take it for granted that he would put it in the net,' Harford commented.

When you suggest to Shearer that the style of play Harford initiated and developed was ideally suited to him, he quickly stresses, 'It was designed to get the best out of all the players, not just me.' However, whether they would have shared that view in the event of Shearer not scoring as many goals as he did, and not being as grounded as a person, is another matter. The fact that, in Harford's words, he was 'a superstar without a superstar's temperament' helped him as much as it did at Southampton. 'The other players loved him,' Harford said. 'I never heard one bad word about him from anybody.'

When I relayed to Harford Jason Dodd's recollection about Shearer not expecting the service to him to be spot on, he immediately provided a similar anecdote. He recalled a Blackburn training session at the start of Shearer's Ewood Park career, part of which was devoted to Shearer making diagonal runs from the middle on to passes behind the opposing full-back. The player responsible for playing the ball was having a bad day, giving Shearer an impossible task by hitting the ball too long or too short. Harford stopped the session, but before he could say anything, Shearer, recognising the problems his colleague was creating for himself through striving for slide-rule accuracy, shouted to the player, 'Look, you don't have to give the perfect ball. As long as you just get it into the right general area, it's up to me to do something with it.' Harford pointed out, 'Some players in Shearer's position would have tried to be smart or had a go at the fellow, but his reaction was to take all the pressure off the player.'

The obvious danger in this was that it almost invited Shearer's team-mates to give him below-par service, which Dalglish found particularly difficult to accept in connection with some of the crosses he was given. But being forced to stretch himself was a situation Shearer relished. His willingness to bust a gut in striving to adjust to different situations and circumstances has been an integral part of his game throughout his career.

Take his relationship with his striking partners. When Blackburn landed the title, his sidekick was Chris Sutton. But Shearer's number-one choice would have been Newell, who was his closest friend at the club and who is still described by Shearer as probably the striker he has most enjoyed playing with at club level. Newell, whom Dalglish had signed in November 1991 and who was Shearer's regular partner until Sutton came along, enjoyed involving himself in the build-up play and got as much enjoyment out of setting up chances for others as he did from scoring himself. Because of his work in deeper areas, Harford described him as a 'half' centre-forward. He was the ideal foil for Shearer – a 'full' centre-forward. It was the same with Teddy Sheringham (like Newell, a 'half' centre-forward) when he and Shearer played together in the England team.

'Centre-halves want to have people to mark,' Newell observed, 'and with Alan right up there and me dropping off him into a deeper position, they had problems straight away. They were so scared of Alan that instead of one of the two central defenders pushing forward on to me they would both stay in there. At times, I couldn't believe the space I was getting and it was good for Alan too, because strange as it might seem, it can be easier to create space for yourself when it's one against two than when there are two of you up front and you are being marked man for man. Ray [Harford] was very keen on me dropping off Alan because when we were defending it gave us another man who could pinch the ball. When the attack broke down, it was amazing the number of times the ball broke into my area. I could have the ball played into me, and turn with it, and that is when the two central defenders were in trouble because Alan would just make a run off them and you would put the ball in for him.

'We could both play, but the big thing was that we knew our strengths. When Blackburn started in the Premiership, a lot of the matches were real physical battles. If we were in trouble away from home, even at home, the ball would be knocked forward long and it would be up to Alan and myself to make something of it. Whether it was a long ball from the full-back or the goalkeeper, we were always in close contact, with one of us going for the ball and the other supporting him. I mean, you can play with some strikers who might be twenty to thirty yards away from you and all you can do is take the ball a bit further forward. But this didn't happen with Alan and myself. We were great friends off the field as well as on it. We looked upon ourselves as a team within a team. It would be wrong to say that Chris didn't try to help Alan. I wouldn't call him a selfish player – he did his bit. But if you think you're being asked to do something which is going to detract from what you believe you are good at, then you're not going to be totally effective. It's the same in any walk of life.'

Harford agreed. 'I always felt that someone like Newell was better for Shearer than a player like Sutton,' he said, 'for the simple reason that Sutton was more focused on scoring. I am not saying that Chris didn't make any chances for Alan – he did. But the problem was that both players were number nines and their natural instincts were to get as far up the pitch as they could. They didn't provide enough depth.' Harford, in fact, disagreed with Dalglish's decision to sign Sutton from Norwich City, for a club-record fee of £5 million, in the 1994 close season. He felt that Sutton, who could also play at centre-half, was more effective in that position. However, he had to concede that there was a lot to be said for Dalglish building up competition for first-team places and increasing his selection options; and Newell, having undergone a knee operation in the summer, was ruled out of action for the start of the championship-winning season anyway.

Though Sutton seemed uneasy about the high expectations that his price tag had created for him, he and Shearer scored thirteen and seventeen goals respectively in Blackburn's first 21 league matches. But Sutton found it difficult to maintain his form: in the second half of the season, Shearer again scored seventeen times, but his partner could manage only two. 'Chris seemed to lose a bit of confidence,' Newell recalled. 'He wasn't going past people and creating chances as he did before, and he was no real help to Alan because of it. Before, it didn't matter if he wasn't going deeper because he was creating chances for Alan in other ways: through his shots or headers that were rebounding to Alan, for example, and his knock-downs.' With the team struggling as well, it seemed almost perverse that Sutton continued to keep Newell out of the starting line-up. But, thanks to Shearer, Blackburn still managed to scrape out results good enough to bring them the league title.

Also at Blackburn then was another striker who has emphasised the strength-through-adversity message, James Beattie. A local lad, born and raised in Darwen, Beattie started his career at Ewood Park but was very much a peripheral figure during his four seasons there as a full-time professional. He made a total of only four league appearances (including three as a substitute), and in the summer of 1998 Blackburn transferred him to Southampton in a part-exchange deal involving Kevin Davies.

In a Southampton team haunted by relegation fears, he marked his first season there with just five goals in 35 matches. But Beattie did get into the England under-21 team, and Southampton's fans, recognising the ways in which he unsettled opposing defences, voted him their Player of the Year. The next season, during which Glenn Hoddle replaced Dave Jones as manager, was virtually a write-off for him, partly because of injury problems.

Then, at the start of the 2000/01 season, Hoddle attempted to sell him to Crystal Palace. 'He got me in his office and said, "I am thinking of selling you to Crystal Palace,"' the striker recalled. 'I remember thinking, "Why?" But before I could say anything, he asked, "What do you want to do?" I just said, "Well, I'm not going to Crystal Palace – no way. I can play in your team, I know I can.' His reaction was, "All right then, show me what you can do."' Hoddle gave him the chance to do so by putting him in the starting line-up for the Saints' sixth match of the season, against Newcastle. Southampton got their first win, and although Beattie didn't score, he justified Hoddle's willingness to give him a reasonable crack of the whip shortly afterwards with a burst of ten goals in as many matches.

Since then, Beattie has been among the leading Premiership scorers and got into the England team. But then, how could it have been otherwise with a striker who has been described as 'Shearer Mark Two', or 'The Chief', as his ex-Southampton boss Gordon Strachan referred to him? It could easily have been Shearer talking when Beattie told me, 'I have always had faith in my ability. You do take knocks, but you can't allow them to set you back. You have to turn them into something positive. You can always find a positive side, no matter what. I was only twenty when Blackburn released me; they did it with one telephone call to me, and my whole family were really upset. I don't know why Blackburn took that decision, but my attitude [to joining Southampton] was, "OK, this is an opportunity for you to prove them wrong." It was the same when Glenn Hoddle wanted to sell me to Crystal Palace. I always used to say that if I kept injury-free and had a decent first-team run I would score at least fifteen goals a season. But in the last two seasons my expectations of myself have got higher. Before a match, I look at the opposing centre-half in the tunnel and think, "There's no way you are going to stop me." That's not being arrogant in any way; it's just the frame of mind I have got into. People might say that I put too much pressure on myself, but I don't see it like that. I enjoy it. It spurs me on.'

Still, there is only one Alan Shearer, as Beattie found out in his struggle to maintain his success.

CHAPTER SEVEN
METHODS OF ATTACK

'As a manager, my attitude is,
"You can pass as much as you want,
but if it's not hurting me,
what does it matter?"'
GORDON STRACHAN

METHODS OF ATTACK

For most teams, it is difficult enough to find the right goalscoring formula. Maintaining it, or making it stronger and more effective, can present even bigger headaches. That is why, during Southampton's home League Cup tie against their arch south-coast rivals Portsmouth on 2 December 2003, the Saints' demonstrative manager Gordon Strachan seemed particularly agitated when James Beattie received the ball with his back to the goal. Strachan thought the world of Beattie. At the same time, he knew that Beattie's first touch could be erratic, so if there wasn't much space for him to manoeuvre the ball it was always on the cards that the flow of the move would be disrupted. On this occasion, Beattie's failure to make the ball instantly obey him was clearly too much for Strachan to bear. Standing on the edge of the technical zone, the manager signalled his frustration by throwing his hands forward from behind his head. He then walked back to the dug-out, shaking his head and muttering. He must have felt like hugging and kissing Beattie later, after the striker had scored the goals that brought Southampton a 2–0 win. But though this was by no means a rare occurrence, it had become increasingly clear that the technical rough edges to Beattie's game, previously hidden because of his physical qualities and scoring success, had started to rebound on him and his team. Indeed, Beattie's experiences epitomised Andy Roxburgh's point about the need for strikers, and the team-mates responsible for creating their scoring chances, to add greater variation to their play.

Even the most successful teams need to keep changing their scoring methods to stay ahead, and this is obviously easier for clubs such as Arsenal, Manchester United and Chelsea – the ones with the money and stature to attract the best players – than it is for the rest. Indeed, over the years, there have been countless examples of teams at the top adding a new dimension to their attacking play with the signing of new strikers, and of the strikers themselves getting better as well.

When Don Revie was Leeds United's manager, their transformation from a dour, somewhat negative team to an exciting, attacking one stemmed partly from the signing of Allan Clarke from Leicester in June 1969 for a then British record fee of £165,000. Leicester, who had reached the FA Cup final the previous season but had been relegated, could no longer offer Clarke the platform he required to keep improving. That Leeds did so was very much to the benefit of both parties. Leeds, who had won the championship for the first time in 1969, largely because of their defence, became more forceful, ingenious and potent at the other end than many can have anticipated.

'I had the time of my life,' Clarke has said. 'I was with great players. I was with winners. I was also confident about my technical ability, but I can honestly say that I worked ten times harder at Leeds than I did at my previous clubs. It wasn't that I didn't want to do this at Leicester and Fulham, but as I was a sort of big fish in a small pond, nobody really challenged me about my approach to the game there. At Leeds, all the players demanded that I pull my weight on behalf of the team. Playing in Europe had a lot to do with my development there as well. But the biggest thing was the way Leeds dominated teams and the number of chances they created. Look, I don't want to make it seem as if goalscoring is easy – it isn't – but at Leeds it was a piece of cake compared with what it had been like at my other clubs. I go back to the number of great players they had. Great players make the game look simple because they play it simple – that's the art of it. No matter what the position in which you received possession, you always had not one player available to take a pass but two or three. So that's another reason why I became a more complete player at Leeds. The best way I can sum it up is to say that I never felt I had to adjust when I played for England. The only instruction I got from Sir Alf Ramsey was, "Play like you do for Leeds." That's all he really ever said to me.'

It is difficult to imagine Leicester ever being able to take Clarke as far as Leeds did. The same could be said of most other clubs. It is rare for a small-town club to have the financial resources that Blackburn had when Alan Shearer fired them to the Premiership title, a crown worn in all the other seasons by Manchester United or Arsenal. Moreover, Blackburn did it when the Premiership was in only its third season and the number of foreign stars bringing greater individual technical expertise to teams was minuscule compared to what it is today. In 1994/95, Blackburn were a typically British team playing in a typically British competition. The bottom line in the Premiership is that money is very much the name of the game, more so than it has ever been at the top level, and 75 per cent of the teams, being more or less in the same financial boat, are effectively playing just for survival. There is so little to choose between them that a team that might have finished at the top of the group in one season, thus creating expectations and hopes of getting into the elite category, can easily find itself struggling to avoid relegation the next.

In his quest to better himself and keep improving, who could blame Shearer for his moves from Southampton to Blackburn and then to Newcastle? The season after Blackburn's championship triumph – Shearer's last at the club – he again scored more than 30 goals. But Blackburn, having curtailed their money-no-object transfer-market shopping policy, could only finish seventh. The feeling that they had previously over-achieved and that it was time for Shearer to move on to a bigger stage was endorsed by the continuation of their slide. By 1999 they were back in the First Division, following a season in which their total number of league goals amounted to just 38.

One wonders what would have happened to Southampton – one of the lowest-scoring teams in the Premiership in recent seasons – if they hadn't had James Beattie. Strachan himself acknowledges that in rehabilitating himself as a manager at Southampton, after being sacked by Coventry, he owed a considerable debt to his centre-forward. 'Instead of the coaching staff motivating him, he motivates us,' he said. 'You can argue that he could be better at this or that, but there comes a point when there is no way you can say anything to him about it because he has worked himself to a standstill.'

When Strachan became manager in October 2001, Southampton were in the relegation zone. Strachan's first step to pull them out of trouble was to make them fitter, which led to their finishing eleventh. Beattie, despite missing three months because of injury, scored twelve league goals that season, just two fewer than the club's leading scorer Marian Pahars. Then, with Pahars forced out of action for almost all of the 2002/03 season, Beattie reached the twenty-goal mark for the first time in his career. His league haul of 23 made him the Premiership's third highest scorer behind Ruud van Nistelrooy and Thierry Henry. With Southampton's second highest scorer, Brett Ormerod, finding the net no more than five times, the team total stood at just 46, but thanks to their excellent defence it was enough to enable them to end up in eighth place – their best-ever Premiership achievement. An even bigger feather in Strachan's cap, of course, was that Southampton's ability to scrape out good results, through their organisation and energy more than anything else, also led them to the FA Cup final against Arsenal.

But after an encouraging start to the 2003/04 season, and Southampton getting themselves as high in the table as fourth at one point, they found themselves heading back to the anonymous mid-table spot many felt was their true habitat. They eventually finished twelfth, and Beattie's goal total – following a run of six in the opening seven games – ended up at a middle-of-the-road twelve in 32 games.

Why? Part of the answer can be found in his highly physical approach to the game (which ultimately led to Strachan leaving him out of the starting line-up for a while to give him a rest). Beattie, 6ft 1in and thirteen stone, has always been noted for his athleticism, fitness and willingness to stretch himself. Recalling his schooldays, and his emergence as a top junior 100-metre freestyle swimmer, he recalled, 'I was able to train on my own for long periods – it was just me and the pool. I was ranked second in the country at one stage, but I wanted to be at the top of the podium and that's what drove me on. In training, I was doing something like 50,000 metres a week, which is quite a lot for a twelve- or thirteen-year-old.' It has been the same story in his football career.

All players need to work hard; but depending on their level of ball skills and the nature of their teams, some have to work harder than others. In Beattie's case, his image as a powerful rather than skilful striker has been a sensitive subject for him, especially with regard to his limited opportunities to make his mark in the England set-up. His five England appearances were all in largely low-key friendlies (against Australia, Serbia and Montenegro, Croatia, Liechtenstein and Denmark); and because of the manager Sven-Goran Eriksson's policy of using all the players in his squad in such games, Beattie wasn't given much time on the field to really show what he could do. Some observers have suggested that Beattie might also have suffered through some of the other England players having doubts about him being on their technical wavelength.

Certainly, after Beattie's last England match, the 3–2 defeat by Denmark on 16 November 2003, the argument that he had not been given the help he needed came over loud and clear in the report of the game on Southampton's official website. Under the headline 'Beattie Shut Out', Dave Hilley wrote, 'James Beattie learnt a valuable lesson about looking after number one. The Saints striker came off the bench at half-time but was seriously starved of service. He rarely received a pass or cross, as for some reason the other England players appeared to cut him out of the game. That was best highlighted on 71 minutes, when Frank Lampard elected to shoot from a tight angle to the right when a pull-back would have left Beattie with a simple finish.' Some contrast to the unselfishness Beattie showed near the end when he spurned a good shooting chance to set up Danny Murphy for a strike that drifted wide. 'It probably went largely unnoticed,' Hilley continued, 'but there was a key moment around the hour mark when Beattie peeled away from his man, making an intelligent run into the box as Joe Cole picked up the ball in the centre of midfield. It was crying out for the sort of telling ball he is supposed to favour and yet he [Cole] chose to go sideways and the moment was lost. That was the story of the game for Beattie.'

Not surprisingly, when I mentioned all this to Beattie he was unwilling to be drawn on the issue. 'I am well aware of it [the report],' he said, 'but I don't want to go into it. Yeah, there were a few times when I felt I should have received the ball, but there's nothing you can do about it.' At club level, though – and particularly in a team like Southampton – Beattie's approach to the game has been welcomed more warmly. 'When Beattie is doing the running he is capable of, it has the effect of wearing defenders down mentally and physically,' Strachan explained. 'That is what he has to do [in order to score goals], he has to grind people down. I think it suits his temperament to do it anyway, and I can relate to that because I was the same as a player. Jock Stein [Scotland's manager] used to say to me, "Pace yourself." But that was no good to me. I had to go flat-out from the first minute; when I tried to regulate it, the game seemed to pass by me and I got taken off.'

Strachan's point about the importance of Beattie pushing himself through the pain barrier appeared to be endorsed by the statistical details of his performances available to Southampton through their use of the high-tech ProZone computer match analysis system. The system, which has become an integral part of the coaching and match preparation work at a number of leading clubs, comprises a video of games with a tracking set-up involving the use of eight to twelve highly placed sensors around the stadium. This provides every bit of information one could possibly wish to know about the movement of every player on the pitch for the entire game. In Beattie's case, the reports he receives about his physical output – incorporating data on his number of 'low-fatigue, moderate-fatigue and high-fatigue' accelerations and decelerations, the amount of ground he covers with 'high-intensity' runs (at three-quarter pace or higher), the overall distances he covers in games and his running speeds – are not in the easy-reading category. To Southampton, however, the overall message is simple.

Take the club report on Beattie in February 2004, comparing his physical output in the first half of the 2003/04 season, when his scoring touch seemed to have deserted him, with that in the same period the previous season, when he achieved his best scoring record. It revealed drops in his average number of accelerations and decelerations (from 117 to 168); the average distances he had covered with high-intensity runs (956.5 metres to 838 metres); and his average total running distances (from 10.57 kilometres to 10.14 kilometres). In some matches, it was pointed out to him, his high-intensity runs had dropped to around the 400-metre mark. The report commented, 'Even though you are performing in the upper limits of the medium to high categories for your position, your average from last season suggests there is more to come from you. It has been noted that when the manager asks for a response from you physically, you respond to great effect. All you can do to improve your scores is to gain more consistency from game to game.' In the section relating to Beattie's speed, it stated, 'Your performances have been slightly below the standard you set last year. We measure your speed during games for two reasons: one, simply to get a picture of how fast you are; and two, to get an idea of your fatigue state on the day of a game. In aspects such as endurance you can push your body through the work, but a tired body simply won't be able to reach the same top speed as a fresh one. As a side, when we work hard we tend to play better, so it is important to maintain a high level in every game.'

To get the best out of Beattie's physical ability, Southampton, inevitably lacking the individual quality that is a feature of the top teams, concentrated on hitting balls into space for him, as opposed to hitting them at him. This might not have helped other members of the team to give him greater scoring support, but as long as he was getting goals regularly, what did it matter? But once the goals dried up, because of a combination of Beattie's tiredness and opponents becoming more competent in countering Southampton's style of play, it was a different story. 'Your methods of attack, of creating chances, depend mainly on the type of strikers you have,' Strachan observed. 'The top strikers know they are judged on their goal records, so their first thought is to get behind a defence – that must be their main aim. But if that isn't on, then OK, they are able to come short to take it to their feet and join in the build-up. If a striker cannot do the latter, then how are you going to keep the move going and bring him back into the picture? When the ball is played up to him, how are you going to persuade the players in deeper positions to keep making the necessary forward runs to support him? If you cannot play off him, the midfielders aren't going to score many goals and the striker you are operating with isn't going to score many goals either.

'Opposing teams are making it more difficult for us to give Beattie the service we want to give him. When they lose the ball deep in our half, they push up on our back men and force us to play through them. James likes to be the furthest man up the park, to take on the last man, but in order to get the ball he is having to come towards it, to the point where sometimes he is virtually on top of it. That's where any problems he might have with his touch and close control can come to the fore. At Coventry we used to force Niall Quinn to do that [in matches against Sunderland]. Instead of hitting the ball straight up to him, they would have to pass it through us. All Quinn could do when he came deep was play it wide, and even then the chances of his being able to get on the end of a cross in the box were minimal.

'James's hold-up play has improved in the time I have been with him at Southampton, and it will continue to do so. He is a wonderful player for a manager or coach to work with. I have given him bollockings, but he's all right with that – he accepts criticism. He is also an intelligent lad, which is probably even more important. He absorbs everything you tell him, and that's why I think he will surprise a lot of people over the next few years. At this stage, though, a lot depends on his fitness. I would say that when he's fit and running well, his technical level goes up to seven or seven and a half out of ten, whereas when he's tired it drops to about four out ten.'

Before the start of the 2003/04 season, Strachan had gone at least some of the way towards varying Southampton's attacking approach and thus increasing their scoring potential with the signing of Kevin Phillips from Sunderland for £3.25 million. Strachan reasoned that Phillips's control and vision in tight areas and his ability to orchestrate Southampton's play in the last third of the field would enable them to become less 'one-dimensional'. Nobody could argue with that logic. However, in the ebb and flow of a game there were bound to be times when the areas in which Phillips excelled would be filled by Beattie. Moreover, Phillips needed the defenders and midfielders to be as comfortable on the ball as he was to be able to properly prove his worth – a situation that was bound to take Southampton time to achieve, if only because of the extent to which the team's previous footballing habits had been ingrained. Sure enough, as Southampton's performances and results became ever more erratic, Strachan was forced to revert to the approach they knew best.

To watch some of Strachan's work behind the scenes at Southampton was to provoke the thought that getting more goals from a team outside the Arsenal–Manchester United–Chelsea axis is often even harder work for the managers and coaches than it is for the players. Their planning for matches is almost like a military operation, with much time being spent analysing the strengths and weaknesses of the opposition through videos and scouting reports and working on ways to deal with them on the training ground. To managers and coaches, the strategic aspect of matches can resemble a game of chess; and what makes it all the more complicated is that many don't have all the pieces.

One example of Strachan's problems in that department was Southampton's home match against Blackburn in October 2003. Southampton had scored only once in their previous six matches, in the 1–1 draw against Steaua Bucharest at home in the first leg of their Uefa Cup tie; Steaua beat them 1–0 in the return leg, and Southampton had also lost 1–0 to Middlesbrough and Newcastle United, and 2–0 to Everton. For the Blackburn game Phillips was unavailable through suspension, and Brett Ormerod, who was generally reckoned to be the next best striking partner for Beattie, was suffering from flu. That left Jo Tessem, whose only previous appearance that season had been as a substitute at Birmingham in August; Leandre Griffit, a nineteen-year-old French striker who had been signed on a Bosman free in the summer but had yet to make his senior debut; and Agustin Delgado, the Ecuador star who had been on the injured list for so long since his move to Southampton in the summer of 2002 that the fans and local media had dubbed him 'The Invisible Man'.

As expected, Strachan opted to work mainly with Beattie and Tessem in his tactical preparations for the game. Pondering his options in his office at Southampton's training ground, he said, 'Not being able to play Kevin is probably the biggest headache. Neither Brett nor Joe have his ability to receive the ball to their feet and play. Joe is reasonably good technically, but he is not strong. So any thoughts we might have of playing the beautiful game on Saturday will have to go out of the window. Our build-up play will have to be more basic.' Strachan then moved over to the 'players' on the magnetic board on his office wall to give some visual examples of how he felt Beattie and Tessem, and the team, could best overcome Phillips's absence. Moving both 'Beattie' and 'Tessem' into central positions, in which they were in close contact with each other, he said, 'When we are attacking, we have to keep the strikers narrow.' He then showed why by moving the discs representing Blackburn defenders towards the pair, and showing the space this created for Beattie and Tessem to run into.

For a while, it seemed that this was going to work only up to a point; Blackburn, with their back four protected by a five-man midfield unit, were able to keep Beattie and Tessem at arm's length. Beattie did get one great chance, a free header, but failed to take it. But three minutes later, with the pressure on Southampton escalating, Beattie had no hesitation in pushing himself forward to take a direct free-kick 25 yards out, and further underlined his tremendous temperament by firing the ball into the net. Beattie, not known as a creator of chances for others, also made the defence-splitting pass from which Griffit, brought on as a substitute for Tessem, made it 2–0.

Despite that victory, Southampton continued to blow hot and cold in attack. Strachan's feeling that he needed to go back to the drawing board became particularly strong after the 1–0 defeat at Aston Villa in November. It was perhaps only to be expected that, as a result of Southampton's attempts to string more passes together than they had the previous season, their number of shots and headers would decline. But after the Villa game Strachan found it impossible to ignore the fact that the home team, despite having made fewer passes than any of Southampton's other Premiership opponents, had created the most chances.

It was at that point that he elected to revert to what he termed 'reality football'. Recalling his experiences in Leeds United's highly successful if not technically sophisticated teams under the management of Howard Wilkinson, he argued, 'You cannot really knock any style of play if it's creating chances. I was brought up in good passing teams [at Aberdeen and Manchester United], but there are times when you have to say that this side of the game – the importance that people attach to it – can be termed propaganda. I'm sure there are plenty of good passing teams who have been relegated. As a manager, my attitude is, "You can pass as much as you want, but if it's not hurting me, what does it matter?"'

All of which took Strachan into which many will have considered territory. Those who did not know him could easily have believed that he had become a disciple of the methods of figures such as Wing Commander Charles Reep and Charles Hughes. Reep, who lived in Torbay and followed his National Service by working for the RAF as an accountant, is generally recognised as having invented the concept of match analysis through statistical data. Hughes, as director of coaching at the Football Association, followed his lead to the point where statistics, especially with regard to the brand of football most likely to produce goals, provided the foundation for the FA's coaching strategies. These are the men who are viewed as having the most to answer on the preoccupation of a high number of teams, both at home and abroad, with the so-called 'long-ball' game, a style of play that has always caused football's most skilful performers to wince.

For Reep, it had all started in the 1950s when he went to watch a match at Swindon and, having logged the number of times they had been in possession of the ball, wondered why it was that they had scored only two goals. He became obsessed with the subject, and embarked on a massive research programme which over the course of some 30 years emphasised two statistical points to him. The first was that the highest number of goals were scored in an area of the field which he described as the PoMO (Position of Maximum Opportunity) sector. As if this was not enough to get teams tuned in to the idea of getting the ball from one end of the field to the other as quickly as possible – not wasting too much energy on weaving pretty patterns with it in order to make sure they retained possession – his other finding was that the smaller the number of passes in an attacking move, the greater its chances of success.

One manager who acted on such information was Stan Cullis, whose Wolves team emerged as one of the most successful in England in the 1950s as a consequence. Another was Graham Taylor, who handed Reep a contract as an adviser during the early part of his career at Watford in the 1980s. Taylor was once quoted as saying, 'Some things [in Reep's teachings] are dangerous. But here is a man who has recorded how goals are scored over more than thirty years. When he throws that number of goals at you, and when you watch it yourself, you say to yourself, "Hey, that fellow's right."' Indeed, under Taylor, Watford burst from the old Fourth Division to the First in five years, and reached the FA Cup final. Wimbledon, using similar methods, rose from non-league football to the First Division in nine years and provided one of the greatest boosts of all time for teams of their indifferent individual technical ability by sensationally beating Liverpool in the 1988 FA Cup final.

For all the criticism directed at managers who have applied the match analysis findings in their purest form – for instance John Beck when he was at Cambridge – most can see the sense of them with teams that have comparatively ordinary or average players. Less easy to accept is the view that the tactics are no less valid for even the most talented of sides. Reep once wrote, 'The time will come when the choice of the manager for the England team will have to be confined to those very few who have a clear understanding of random chance in soccer and who have exploited it successfully.' When I once interviewed Hughes, he pointed out that even in matches involving the top teams, the vast majority of goals came from no more than five passes, usually from counter-attacks stemming from possession regained in the last third of the field. His message was that even in a World Cup final a team getting the ball forward as quickly as possible and pushing up to compress the play would have the best chance of victory. He saw no reason why this should not form the main part of player coaching sessions. Referring to the development of schoolboy players, he said, 'They need not just more practice, but more practice on the things that will pay the highest dividends. In any sport, people practise hard to increase their chances of winning. They don't practise to lose.' Then came the disturbing bit: Hughes's assertion that Brazil's players wasted their dazzling skills by being too self-indulgent. 'Even Brazil have scored most of their goals with five passes or fewer, so it follows that had they adhered to this more slavishly, their results would have been even better.'

Strachan was never liable to go that far. Nonetheless, in his attempts to halt Southampton's slide you could appreciate why he saw no reason to be embarrassed about getting back to basics. In a club website interview, he said, 'I was looking for a bit more variation in our play this season, but I was possibly asking them [the players] to do things they were not comfortable with. Maybe some of them aren't ready to take that step forward. At this stage, we are brilliant at being ordinary and playing from the heart, and through that comes our ability. We are now going back to what we were. We will still work on the other things in training, so when the time is right we can introduce them gradually. But for now, we will stick with what works for us.'

Portsmouth, in their League Cup tie at Southampton, became the first team to feel the full force of this. Strachan, as he showed when Beattie was on the ball, still fretted about his side's inability to retain possession. But the other side of the coin was the way in which Portsmouth were undermined by his centre-forward's power and determination. After 33 minutes, Ormerod suddenly put Portsmouth in difficulty by taking the ball off a defender and putting Chris Marsden clear down the left. Marsden crossed hard and low, and Beattie, attacking the ball as if his life depended on getting to it, put it in the net. In injury time, Beattie's will to score was seen again as he forced himself in between two defenders. The only way one of them, Arjan De Zeeuw, was able to stop him was to bring him down, a foul that led to the big Dutchman being sent off and Beattie converting the penalty.

So there were no prizes for guessing the name of the Southampton player that Charlton, the Saints' next opponents, thought about the most in their preparations for the game. When I visited their training ground three days before the match, Charlton's coach, Mervyn Day, and the manager, Alan Curbishley, were discussing Beattie's performance against Portsmouth as they were walking on to the pitch with their squad. There hadn't seemed anything especially riveting about Beattie's opening goal; after all, it was from close in and he did have virtually an unguarded target. Curbishley, though, referring to the way in which Beattie attacked the ball, was struck by his apparent hunger to score. 'You could almost see it in his eyes,' he said.

Later, Day expressed his admiration for Phillips as well. 'We wanted him desperately [when Sunderland agreed to sell him in the summer] and he badly wanted to come here,' he said. 'But at that time we just couldn't raise the money. Phillips and Niall Quinn complemented each other perfectly at Sunderland, and Phillips and Beattie also complement each other at Southampton. You often find good striking duos like those, where the two strikers are total opposites. You rarely get two the same. That's not to say that you don't want both to score, but as long as one is getting a lot of goals, it doesn't matter. I do like striking partnerships like this.'

Phillips hadn't played against Portsmouth because of tonsillitis, but Day and Curbishley both felt he would be back in the starting line-up for Charlton's visit to St Mary's Stadium. This became particularly clear as Day, who takes on most of the responsibility for organising Charlton's defence, supervised the customary training match involving the first-team keeper and back-four players against a group of attacking players replicating the styles of play of those at Southampton. Charlton have named these sessions 'Stars in Your Eyes' – a reference, of course, to the ITV variety programme hosted by Matthew Kelly. On this occasion one didn't need to think long and hard to deduce that the tall, powerfully built Charlton player at centre-forward (their Swedish striker Jonatan Johansson) and the short one operating with him up front (a youth-team player) were filling the roles of 'Beattie' and 'Phillips'. Charlton's left-back, Chris Powell was on the right flank because Powell is a natural left-footed player, the same as Southampton's French right-side midfielder Fabrice Fernandes, whose balls into the box (with his left foot) had proved one of Southampton's most effective attacking assets. Also included in that training session were the sort of long throw-ins propelled into opposing goal areas by The Saints' Rory Delap.

Because of Beattie's ability in the air, especially when the ball is played to the far post, it was no less interesting to note the positional changes among Charlton's back four. In normal cirumstances, their line-up would have been Radostin Kishishev at right-back, Chris Perry and Mark Fish at the heart of the defence, and Hermann Hreidarsson at left-back. The plan against Southampton was for Perry and Fish to swap sides. Why? Day explained that in the usual set-up, the positions on the right side of Charlton's defence were filled by the smallest of the defenders. 'So if I was manager or coach of Southampton,' he added, 'I would be telling our team to keep getting the ball to Fernandes and I would tell Beattie to keep getting

175

in between Kishishev and Perry [for the far-post cross].' The positional changes meant that the line-up in terms of height changed from 5ft 11in–5ft 9in–6ft 4in–6ft 3in to 5ft 11in–6ft 3in–5ft 9in–6ft 4in. 'Obviously their main scoring threat at the moment is Beattie,' Day continued, 'and we have concentrated on that threat. When Southampton are in the final third they put a lot of crosses into the box and he attacks them very well. Today has been about getting our back four in the right positions – hopefully the right positions! – to deal with it. Beattie is a strong runner, he can get behind you, but the main priority is to nullify his ability in the air. That means defending higher up the pitch when the ball is in crossing areas. When Fernandes checks back and crosses the ball with his left foot, you want the back four holding the line; the last thing you want is for them to drop back to the six-yard box. You have to force him to head the ball from sixteen or seventeen yards out, as opposed to six or eight yards out.

'I think you will find that if they are going to play into feet, they are going to play into Phillips's feet, not Beattie's. They will play down the sides for Beattie [hit direct passes into space for him so that he can run with it towards the goal]. If the ball is played up to him, he's not the type who finds it natural to turn with it, so you can afford to get quite tight on him and pressurise his first touch. If he gets turned and is running at you, then it's important to shove him on to his left foot and force him away from the goal. Above all, we have to work hard enough to cut out a lot of the service to him.'

This led Day on to the subject of Strachan's comment about 'passing propaganda'. Day, once Strachan's team-mate at Leeds, said, 'People said Leeds were a long-ball team, which they were. But what was wrong was the stigma attached to this. A long ball does not necessarily mean a crude whack up the field. A quality fifty-yard ball is better than a quality ten-yard ball because the fifty-yard one takes you forty yards further up the field. When it comes to creating scoring chances, it must be an advantage to get into the last third of the field quicker.

'As you get higher in the league, you need better players [to provide greater variation]. You cannot stand still. I do sometimes think that you can make existing players better just through a change of system, but I can see where Gordon is coming from. The ways you attempt to create scoring chances depend on the strengths of your players. It suits Southampton to hit the front men as early as they can, partly because they are an exceptionally fit team – as Leeds were – and they have the legs to get up and back. We have to match that.'

Unfortunately for Charlton, things didn't work out as they had anticipated. It all started to go wrong for them when Fish was taken ill just before kick-off and had to be replaced by the comparatively inexperienced Jonathan Fortune. Also, Beattie again lined up alongside Ormerod and not Phillips, and Fernandes had to make way for Pahars. The changes seemed to make Southampton stronger than ever. Having established a 2–0 lead and then been pulled back to 2–2 through two outstanding shots from Scott Parker, they finally won 3–2. Perhaps the most surprising aspect of the victory was that Beattie didn't score (Rory Delap got the first goal with a deflected shot and Ormerod the other two). It was the first home match Southampton had won without any goals from him for fourteen months.

However, Beattie did do much to undermine Charlton in other ways. One of his best moments came just before half-time when his tenacity in chasing an apparently over-hit pass from David Prutton through the inside-right channel enabled him to just keep it in play. Then, as if to disprove the notion that he is not the best at setting up chances for others, he pulled the ball back for Ormerod to score Southampton's second goal. He was also involved in the Saints' third goal, taking advantage of Charlton's failure to properly clear a Jason

Dodd corner with a headed pass that led to Michael Svensson giving Ormerod the opportunity to get the winner. 'Today was the first time this season that we have been a threat every time we have got the ball,' Strachan said. 'In defence, which we don't practise that much, we have been nine out of ten, but attacking-wise, we have only been five out of ten. Today, I think we were up to nine out of ten.'

There were other Southampton performances for Strachan to savour before his departure from the club in March 2004 (a parting of the ways arising from the decision by Strachan himself not to remain there beyond the end of the season). But with the physical strain on Beattie having caught up with him, and his team still inconsistent, it seemed that Southampton had run into a brick wall.

Strachan and Southampton had come a long way together. No doubt, in addition to his feeling that he needed to take a break from the pressures of management, his reluctance to sign the new contract that had been offered to him also stemmed from doubts about whether it was possible to take the club further under their exisiting financial structure. It was tempting to suggest that in order to make the step from being a middle-of-the-table team to a good top-half one Southampton needed to loosen their purse strings in the transfer market. At the same time, in view of the horrendous financial problems Leeds have experienced, one could understand why the Saints' chairman Rupert Lowe, in common with many of his counterparts, was sensitive about the dangers of his club trying to live beyond its financial means.

Perhaps one consoling thought for Southampton, and all the other teams striving to improve their scoring ability, was that even Arsenal did not have everything. Even during a season in which the Gunners became the first top-level team in modern times (and only the second in the history of English football) to go through the season with no league defeats, some professional observers felt that they occasionally missed not having a conventional centre-forward. Their argument was that a big, strong number 9 who was good in the air and could create problems for the opposition in the physical sense, would have provided an invaluable extra dimension to their build-up play in periods when their close-passing and dribbling skills were not working.

Who could have given them that option? One of the names put forward was James Beattie.

CHAPTER EIGHT
SHARING THE LOAD

'Players [non-strikers] have got to
have the confidence to go and score goals.
They need to go out on the pitch
believing they can score and be ready to
take responsibility rather than
maybe leaving it to the front two.'

PAUL STURROCK

A ll managers argue that, while it is mainly the strikers' job to score goals, the responsibility should be spread throughout the team. In recent seasons, the advantages of this have been borne out particularly spectacularly by David Beckham's free-kick goals and, at the less skilful end of the English football scale, Plymouth Argyle's achievement in becoming the highest-scoring team in the country.

Who can ever forget the 30-yard Beckham free-kick in the last minute of England's World Cup qualifying tie against Greece, which gave England a 2–2 draw and an automatic place in the 2002 finals? Getting the ball in the net from outside the penalty area (not just from free-kicks but also in open play) was also Peter 'Hot Shot' Lorimer's speciality during his Leeds United career. The right winger or right-side midfielder who was Leeds' record post-war league scorer might not have been able to bend it like Beckham, but the power and accuracy of his long-range shots was awesome. He once said, 'It was a great thing to have in your attacking armoury. Your team could be in trouble, but suddenly they'd get a free-kick and – bang. They were level or ahead, and you were a hero.

'In those days, it [the art of converting free-kicks] was mostly about power. You could not make the ball bend and dip – the balls were heavier than the ones used now when the conditions were wet and muddy – but this was no handicap to me. Sometimes I would blast the ball straight at the keeper, and other players would pick up goals from the rebounds. We knew it was unlikely that the keeper would be able to hold the ball, so when I hit it we would have two or three players in specific areas around him to pick up the pieces. Most of the goals I scored in open play came from long range. Like Eddie Gray [Leeds' left winger], I used to pick the ball up deep and go at people. Once I was over the halfway line, maybe thirty to forty yards from goal, I would start thinking, "Goal here." It was quite funny sometimes because just as people were starting to give you stick for not passing to them – and it usually came from the strikers – the ball would be flying into the top corner of the net. So then it would be OK.'

Plymouth did not have a Lorimer or a Beckham when they won the Second Division title in the 2003/04 season. But this wasn't of much consolation to the defences they faced because they had all the other elements necessary to get plenty of goals from non-strikers. Managed for the most part by Paul Sturrock, who was to become Gordon Strachan's replacement at Southampton, Plymouth (unlike Southampton) had an outstanding target-man centre-forward in Micky Evans; and the vast majority of Plymouth's work in training was based on getting defenders and midfielders into scoring positions.

Of course, there is a world of difference between the Second Division of the Nationwide League and the Premiership. But it was interesting to note that while Southampton's league goal haul was 44 in 38 matches, Plymouth, with Evans the top scorer among their central strikers on just twelve, got 85 goals in 46 matches. During

Sturrock's time there, they never relied as heavily on one player, and especially a striker, to get their goals as Southampton had on Beattie. In their 2001/02 Third Division championship-winning season, Plymouth's most prolific scorer was their central defender Graham Coughlan, with eleven; the only front man able to present a serious challenge to him was Marino Keith, who was in second place on nine. Keith did manage to regain some of his self-respect by being the only double-figure scorer the following season, but his total of eleven was only three higher than that of Coughlan's central defensive partner Paul Wotton. In the 2003/04 season, their top scorer was midfielder David Friio with fourteen. Apart from Evans, Keith had to share the third spot with Wotton on nine.

No central defender has established a scoring reputation quite like that of Daniel Passarella, the inspirational captain of Argentina's 1978 World Cup-winning team. Passarella was the defender who scored the highest number of goals in the Argentinian League and Italy's Serie A. It was the same story at international level, where his record was 22 in 70 matches. Although he was only 5ft 9in, Passarella, strong and athletic, scored a high number of goals with his head.

The most obvious way in which central defenders can get in on the scoring act is through set-piece moves. Almost all of them are good in the air, and the routines managers and coaches come up with to bring them into the picture at indirect free-kicks and corners are many and varied. Central defenders can also find the net in open play, of course, especially if they are in the mould of Colin Hendry (the former Blackburn and Scotland centre-half who seemed to perform at times as if hypnotised into believing he was the centre-forward); and, most importantly, they can time their runs into scoring positions properly.

It is in the latter respect that attacking midfielders come into their own as scorers. As Sturrock said, 'I have always found that the late runs into the box are the hardest for teams to defend against.' In the past, midfielders running off their markers and taking advantage of the attention of opposing defenders being focused on the strikers has been particularly well illustrated by the remarkable scoring records of men such as Martin Peters at Tottenham and West Ham in the 1960s and 1970s, and John Wark at Ipswich and Liverpool in the 1970s and 1980s.

Peters, nicknamed 'The Ghost' because of his ability to sneak virtually unnoticed into finishing positions, was probably the first player in England to truly bring this facet of the game to the fore. There wasn't much that Peters could not do on a football field. Indeed, the footballing intelligence and wide range of skills that enabled him to fill a multitude of different positions or roles at West Ham prompted his England manager, Sir Alf Ramsey, to come out with that famous comment about Peters being 'ten years ahead of his time'. Ramsey meant it as the ultimate compliment. It stemmed from the manager's vision of teams of the future being packed with players interchanging positions, the sort of players for which Ajax were to become renowned when their 'total' football swept them to three successive European Cup triumphs at the start of the 1970s. For his part, though, Peters was initially touchy about the comment because at that time he viewed his versatility as a handicap. In his 1975 autobiography, aptly titled *Goals from Nowhere*, he wrote that he 'detested' being described in his early days at West Ham as a 'utility' player. 'Do you know where the term "utility man" comes from?' he complained. 'It's an old theatrical term which, my dictionary explains, means "an actor employed to play unimportant parts, when required".'

His turning point came when he was left out of the West Ham team for their 1965 European Cup Winners' Cup final win over Munich 1860, and demanded to the manager, Ron Greenwood, that he be given a more clearly defined role. Greenwood eventually gave him the job of hunting for goals from the 'hole' just behind the strikers. Even then it bothered Peters that the subtlety with which he did his job – the fact that much of his work boiled down to intelligent but largely unnoticed runs off the ball – caused him to be underrated by the general public. As for that comment by Ramsey, he said, 'It looked at first to be the sort of thing someone says about you before they show you the door. But the longer I thought about it, the more I saw that not only was it a compliment, but that it gave me an identity. Heaven knows how badly I needed one. I felt that an awful lot of people who watched me play for West Ham and England did not have the faintest idea what I was supposed to be doing out there. And because they were vague about me they were vague about whether I was really necessary.' The answer to that was provided by his scoring record. Quite apart from the part he played in England's 1966 World Cup triumph, his new role at West Ham brought him 100 goals in 364 matches, including a career-best total of 24 in 48 in the 1967/68 season.

John Wark, initially a centre-half, did not have Peters' talent, but through his strength and power, and his scoring instincts, his record as a midfielder-striker was even more impressive. Wark is best remembered for his amazing exploits in the 1980/81 season, when he scored 36 goals, including fourteen (then a record) in the Uefa Cup. More recently, the most highly-rated Premiership scorer among those not filling conventional central striking roles has been Manchester United's Paul Scholes.

In taking some of the scoring pressure off the strikers, men such as Peters, Wark and Scholes have done much to mirror the changes in the basic playing 'shapes' or systems of teams. The earliest of these basic patterns, in the 1880s, was the 2–2–6 formation. These days, the most common line-up, certainly at the top levels, is 4–5–1 or

4–4–1–1. How did we get to this? In the tactical 'numbers game' played by managers and coaches, 2–2–6 was followed by 2–3–5 and then the WM formation, which could be said to be basically 3–2–2–3. The extra man at the back arose as a result of the 1925 change in the offside law, which meant that to remain onside a striker in the most advanced attacking position needed to have only one outfield opponent in front of him, not two, when he received the ball. With most teams still using only two men as their last line of defence (they were ostensibly full-backs), with the centre-half further forward alongside two 'wing-halves', the change inevitably led to a higher number of goals.

Ironically, the decision by teams to increase the number of players at the back, by moving the centre-half there, has been attributed partly to the Sunderland and Arsenal forward Charlie Buchan. Newcastle, one leading team that did take up the idea of a three-man defence and became recognised as the masters of the offside game as a result, beat Arsenal 7–0, and legend has it that Buchan was so incensed about it that he persuaded the Gunners' manager, Herbert Chapman, to follow Newcastle's example. It was therefore Arsenal, as a result of their emergence in the 1930s as the most dominant team in England, who did the most to make this defensive line-up so common.

The writing on the wall for the WM shape, indeed for any system in which players do not adjust, became particularly clear when England suffered their first-ever home defeat against Hungary at Wembley in 1953. As the Hungarians adopted a 4–2–4 structure, England's three-man defence was often outnumbered and it conceded six goals. Not only this, Hungary's centre-forward Nandor Hidegkuti did not operate in the way England's centre-half Billy Wright had come to expect of number 9s. In today's parlance, Hidegkuti seemed more like an attacking midfielder than a striker.

Some years later, Wright wrote, 'He was the one who really won it for Hungary. Others, like Puskas [who scored a hat-trick], got more credit, but it was Nandor who pulled us all over the place and opened up the gaps. No one had put the centre-forward as deep as that before. Don Revie did the same thing later with Manchester City. It made a big difference to the English game. No longer was it relevant to take much notice of the numbers on players' shirts.' So 4–2–4 became the next system to come into football fashion. Then came 4–3–3, 4–4–2 and formations such as 4–5–1 that have given birth to the so-called 'lone striker' role.

As that England team failed to appreciate against Hungary, systems, like statistics, can be interpreted in a number of different ways. None of them is cast in stone; they can all change a great deal during a game. For example, if you are playing Manchester United, Arsenal or Chelsea, your 3–5–2 is inclined to be more like 5–3–2 (or even 5–5–0 if you are a poor team!). In the space of 90 minutes the shape of a team can alter so many times that most spectators trying to work out what is going on could easily end up reaching frantically for the aspirin bottle. However, the way in which the team systems have evolved does show that strikers getting help from other members of the team has become increasingly important.

One explanation for teams cutting the number of men in their front line, and increasing the number in the midfield zone, is that it increases their chances of retaining possession and controlling the play, and makes it more difficult for the opposition to penetrate them. These factors are viewed as being of paramount importance in matches involving the most skilful and accomplished teams. No less pertinent is the fact that teams, conscious of the uneasiness of defenders when they don't have anybody specifically to mark, have become increasingly attached to the idea of having potential scorers in areas in which their goal threat is less apparent.

In his book 'Flat Back Four: Tactics of Football', Andy Gray, looking at the pros and cons of 4–3–3, 4–4–2 and 4–5–1 from a striker's point of view, wrote, 'Three up front is harder to work as a front man [than two up front] because you have to be more disciplined. You are much more limited as to where you can go. When you just have two, you are always interchanging; it is less regimented and harder for defenders to work out what you are doing. In modern-day football, the hardest thing about playing as a [conventional] striker is finding space. Defences are so well organised that trying to break them down can be like banging your head against a brick wall, which is why a lot of teams play with one up and one off [in the space just behind]. One thing that defenders hate above all is players who run at them with the ball, and that's what the player in the "hole" does.'

As Gray said, some lone strikers are more isolated than others, which goes some way towards explaining the difference between 4–5–1 and 4–4–1–1. For example, Eric Cantona was looked upon as a 'hole' player when he was with Manchester United, but as Gray pointed out, even when United were in possession the Frenchman spent much of his time 'scurrying around near the centre circle'. But, on the general principle of a striker being up front on his own, Gray argued that it was essential for his team to be able to play through the midfield and have team-mates in deeper positions quickly supporting him. 'There is no point in knocking endless long balls to a player on his own up front. It's too big a job for him to protect the ball. It's a strange role for a striker, because he becomes more of a creator around the box than a finisher.'

The job clearly created problems for Alan Shearer when Terry Venables subjected him to the lone-striker role, as part of his 'Christmas Tree' 4–5–1 system, with the England team in the mid-1990s. Venables said, 'David Platt and Peter Beardsley [the most attack-minded of England's midfield five] are essentially functioning as forwards so I don't think Shearer is left isolated up front any more than Ian Rush was for Liverpool when they were at their best, or any more than Shearer is with Blackburn. Obviously it's a great advantage for attackers to come into the box from deeper positions because they arrive facing the goal, which creates more options for them and for the man who is already there.' Outside the arguments that the styles of Shearer and Beardsley were simply not compatible, and that perhaps Beardsley was thinking more as a midfielder than a striker, Gary Lineker argued that Shearer had to take much of the blame for his struggle to come to terms with the system.

In an article for the *Observer* newspaper, Lineker, discussing his experience of operating with Beardsley in England's matches in the 1990 World Cup finals in Italy, wrote, 'Some of you may argue that England nearly reached the World Cup final playing with two strikers. The truth is, Peter Beardsley has never been a genuine front man and he was more a link between midfield and me up front.' He added, 'There is no questioning the Blackburn goal machine's [Shearer's] commitment or, indeed, his talent, but the forward's function in this England team requires more thought than effort. In the white shirt of England, Shearer continues to make the runs into wide areas that he does for his club. He does this with total honesty, believing he is helping his team. Without the support of a fellow striker, what he is in fact doing is distancing himself from his team-mates. The build-up should be through the team, with Shearer staying central and attached to his team, enabling him to be used like a wall to bounce the ball off. His runs directly towards goal should only be made when the teams are well into the opposing half.'

In Shearer's defence, Ray Harford told me, 'It goes against the grain for Alan to curtail his running. He likes to play to his physical limits, and I think it's important to him to be seen to be doing that.

Also, the more isolated you are up front, the more you need to have good acceleration. There are times when you have to virtually stand still, and then suddenly go to quick and then lightning quick. He doesn't have that change of pace, and the only way he can compensate for it is to keep on the move and maintain the highest momentum he can.'

It might also have gone against the grain for Shearer to sacrifice some of his scoring instincts, although the view that the odds are heavily stacked against lone strikers getting a lot of goals hardly seemed to stand up in the case of Ruud van Nistelrooy when he was the Champions League's top scorer in the 2002/03 season. And it certainly didn't in the case of Clive Allen at Tottenham in the 1986/87 season.

That was David Pleat's first season as Spurs manager, and in addition to Allen the other attacking players at his disposal included Glenn Hoddle, Ossie Ardiles and Chris Waddle. If Pleat's decision to opt for a 4–5–1 framework was meant to get the best out of any one player, it was Hoddle. The extravagantly gifted England midfielder had always maintained that he needed a free attacking role, one without too many defensive responsibilities, and giving him the support of an extra midfielder seemed the ideal way to grant his wish. The midfield five were in a diamond shape, with Ardiles at the top point – the one closest to the defence – and Hoddle at the bottom point (closest to Allen). Pleat recalled, 'Ardiles would be the one to start off attacks and Hoddle was like the second striker. He did not get a lot of goals himself, but because of his superb passing ability he became the supplier and provider. When people made forward runs from midfield he would often be the one to put them in.'

But it was Allen, very much a goal-poacher – a penalty-box 'ferret', as Pleat described him – who benefited the most. Of course, Allen, too, didn't have to get involved in too much defensive work.

Moreover, apart from having the likes of Hoddle to take the attention of opposing defenders away from him, he didn't have to worry about another striker limiting his positional options. As Pleat explained, 'We gave him the full width of the penalty box – 44 yards across – to work in. We did not want him running into corners, we wanted him to poach. The system gave opposing central defenders a problem. The number 5 would mark Allen, but the number 6 would have to decide whether to cover him or push in on Hoddle.'

Allen, the son of the former Tottenham and England striker Les, loved it. He ended up scoring 33 of Tottenham's total of 68 league goals, which was just four short of the Jimmy Greaves club record of 37 established 24 seasons earlier. Greaves's total in all competitions, 44, was also a record, but Allen smashed that with an overall goal haul of 49. In fact, he was the only Spurs player to get into double figures. That season, Spurs finished third in the First Division, reached the FA Cup final and were League Cup semi-finalists.

As it happens, Paul Sturrock also gave an excellent account of himself as a lone striker in a number of European matches for Dundee United. Thanks to the outstanding knowledge and coaching skills of their manager, Jim McLean, that club – traditionally not even the biggest in Dundee let alone Scotland – repeatedly belied their limited financial resources; and what Sturrock learnt there as one of McLean's leading 'protegés' clearly came in handy at Plymouth.

When I talked to Sturrock about Plymouth's impressive scoring record, before his move to Southampton in March 2004, he said that the starting point for it had come at the end of the 2002/03 season when a review of the club's training schedules prompted him to put a greater emphasis on full-sided training games. Previously, Plymouth had put on a lot of small-sided matches, on half the pitch, to help improve the players' control and close-passing skills, but Sturrock felt that this had been taken to the extreme and had caused his team to become too narrow-minded. 'In the context of the sort of football that is played in the Second Division, the full-sided matches gave us more game-related situations,' Sturrock told me. 'I thought we badly needed to open up our play more.' He deemed it even more important for Plymouth to get in more crosses. 'If there is one thing I know [about the art of teams scoring a lot of goals] it's that crosses into the box are the be all and end all,' he said. 'That's how most goals are scored, and it's something we work exceptionally hard on in training.'

As he pointed out, it was not merely coincidental that Manchester United were looked upon as being at their attacking best when they had David Beckham, arguably the best crosser of the ball in the world, on their right flank – notably in the 1999/2000 season when United, with Ryan Giggs on the other wing and a potential scorers' list that included Paul Scholes, Andy Cole, Dwight Yorke, Ole Gunnar Solskjaer and Teddy Sheringham, established their Premiership scoring record of 98 goals. In that particular season, the breakdowns of United's goals revealed that Beckham had set up almost 40 per cent of them.

One of Sturrock's main priorities before the start of the season was to find players who could make Plymouth as dangerous on the left as they had been on the right. This was achieved with the signings of Peter Gilbert on loan from Birmingham and Tony Capaldi on a free transfer from the Midlands club. 'We were very much a right-sided team before,' Sturrock said. 'Although Martin Phillips is a left-footed player, I have preferred to use him on the right because he seems to put in better crosses from there. He's a bit like Fabrice Fernandes [at Southampton]. I ended up playing David Norris [a right-footed player] on the left, and he did quite well for me considering that he was totally out of position. But I just felt we got nothing from that side. The signings of Gilbert and Capaldi changed that. We are much better balanced than we were last season. We are getting in loads of crosses from both sides.'

This was not reflected by the scoring records of Plymouth's strikers – a list that comprised Keith and Evans (Sturrock's first-choice front men), Stonebridge, Lowndes and Sturrock's son, Blair. Keith was the only member of the group whom Sturrock said could be classified as a natural goalscorer (on the grounds that he was more of a penalty-box player than the others and more single-minded about scoring), and Keith's finishing could be somewhat erratic. This, though, did not matter to Sturrock because all the others were superior to Keith in helping to set up chances for others, the 31-year-old Evans especially. 'He has been the most influential striker in the Second Division this season,' Sturrock said. 'His scoring ability has improved. Micky was a poor mover in the box before. If the ball was about to be crossed, he would just sort of position himself by the back post and wait for it. You needed radar to find him. Now he's on the move all the time – back post, front post – and he's reaping the benefit. But that is only part of the story with him this season. Just as important to us is that he can hold the ball up and see a pass. When we need him to do that, it doesn't mean he cannot score: if he knocks the ball wide there's no reason why he cannot get into the box and be on the end of the cross. But the main thing is that he has helped to take us forward and given others the scope to put the ball in the net, if not himself. The way Micky has linked our play has been superb. You can bang the ball up to him from the back knowing that it will rarely come back. We work on statistics, and these show that as much as 68 per cent of all the passes that have been played up to our front men have been held. I would say that Micky has been mainly responsible for that.'

195

To put it another way, it was Evans who could take much of the credit for Plymouth repeatedly being able to bring their wide men into play and, in turn, the midfielders being able to start thinking about making those runs to get on the end of their crosses. 'David Friio created the biggest headaches for defences because he could leave it so late,' Sturrock said. The most stunning example of Plymouth's overall scoring power was the 7–0 win over struggling Chesterfield – their biggest home victory since 1936. Sturrock ranked Plymouth's first-half display, when they scored five goals in the opening seventeen minutes and six by the interval, as the best by any team he had managed. The other reason why the match stood out in his memory was that all but two of the goals came from midfielders. Friio, with two headers from corners and a shot from a headed knockdown by Evans, became the first Plymouth player to get a hat-trick in more than three years. Lee Hodges and Tony Capaldi also found the net.

Upon joining Southampton, Sturrock said: 'Players [non-strikers] have got to have the confidence to go and score goals. They need to go out on the pitch believing they can score and ready to take responsibility rather than maybe leaving it to the front two. Maybe not enough players go out looking to score. They have to have that mindset, and that is something we will work on.' Prior to his arrival, only two goals had come from players in the Saints' midfield section, but on 27 March, in Sturrock's third match as manager, it became three with the extraordinary overhead kick by Rory Delap that brought the new boss his first Southampton win, 1–0 over Tottenham.

Delap, signed for a club-record fee of £4 million from Derby County in the 2002 close season, is noted for his versatility. He filled every outfield position at Derby, including that of striker, and was even their leading scorer at one point. So why was it that his goal against Spurs was his first of the season, and only his third in some 80 matches for the club? Part of the reason was that Southampton often used him at left-back. Moreover, Sturrock suggested that as a midfielder he tended to try to take on too many responsibilities. The manager liked to think that he helped Delap get on the scoresheet by giving the club's eighteen-year-old French player Yoann Folly his first-team debut in a midfield anchor role, thus providing Delap with greater attacking freedom and 'simplifying' his game.

In the next Southampton match, the 4–1 win at Wolves, their Norwegian centre-half Claus Lundekvam scored his first goal, with a header from a Fernandes free-kick, in 296 competitive matches in English football. Phillips scored twice and Beattie got the other, but for obvious reasons, Sturrock seemed to become particularly animated when talking about Lundekvam. 'He is usually a decoy,' Sturrock pointed out. 'He may as well wear a duck on his head because he is never normally on the end of things. He has to appreciate that he is not just there to drag opponents out of position to give others a scoring chance; that he has to try and score himself. I have been chipping away at him over the last couple of weeks, and he has responded in the right way.'

Of course, Delap and Lundekvam still have a long way to go to match David Friio and Paul Wotton. Still, in taking some of the scoring pressure off Southampton's strikers, at least they started moving in the right direction.

CHAPTER NINE
PROVING THE TALENT-SPOTTERS WRONG

'It's important to be able to accept criticism. I look upon myself as an "old-school" striker because, no matter how much success I might have achieved, I don't want to be mollycoddled.'

DION DUBLIN

PROVING THE TALENT-SPOTTERS WRONG

It's not just their goals that make the top scorers major assets, it's also their saleable value. When clubs run into financial trouble (a common occurence nowadays) the transfers of these players represent their best chance of getting out of it. So the importance of the men responsible for bringing them to the clubs in the first place, notably the managers and the chief scouts, cannot be overstated.

One would think that the job should be relatively straight-forward, given the obvious guidelines to the ability of strikers provided by their scoring records. But the competition to sign them is more intense than it is for players in other positions; and the demands of their roles as they go higher on the football ladder mean many other assessment factors have to be taken into account. For strikers, the development process embodies all manner of potential banana skins, and in overcoming them, some have made professional observers appear the biggest of mugs. Indeed, football is littered with many cases of strikers who one way or another have proved clubs wrong; and, of course, that in itself is a pretty powerful reason for all strikers to keep believing that they can earn decent livings from the game.

Because of the traditional physical nature of the British game, clubs searching for schoolboy strikers to sign have always believed in including the builds and physical strength of the players among their key terms of reference. One of the most famous instances of this backfiring was Aberdeen's mistake in the mid-1950s in not signing a striker who went on to prove arguably the greatest player ever to be born and raised in their area – Denis Law. Aberdeen are hardly in one of the traditional football 'hot-beds' and their scouting network in those days was not as rigorous as it was to become when Alex Ferguson took over as manager in 1978. Even so, not giving Law the chance to start his career there was a boob they have never totally lived down.

In truth, many clubs would have found Law an easy player to overlook. As a boy, he gave the impression that he could easily be blown over by a puff of wind. In addition to his frail-looking build, he wore glasses – the uncool, obtrusive National Health type – to correct a squint. He was only able to play for his school team on the basis of a letter from his mother giving permission for him to take them off.

Law was fourteen when he was brought to Huddersfield Town's attention, thanks to their manager, Andy Beattie, who had been born and raised in Aberdeenshire and had a brother who did some scouting for him there. Beattie once said that his first reaction on meeting Law was that his brother was trying to play a practical joke on him. However, the more he saw Law in action, the more he appreciated how deceptive appearances can be. To Beattie, Law's physique could easily be worked on and improved. In the meantime, Law, with his fiery, combative personality, was not the type to allow defenders to walk all over him; on top of this came his hunger for success and those razor-sharp scoring instincts.

Bill Shankly, Huddersfield's assistant manager when Law was

signed by the club, was also enthusiastic about his potential. So much so that Shankly's appointment as Beattie's successor led to Law being given his league debut at the age of just sixteen, a club record. Two years later, Law became the youngest player to be capped by Scotland. For Aberdeen, the agony continued with Law's transfers – all for record fees – to Manchester City, Manchester United and Torino. Such was his impact at United that to this day he is known among their followers as 'The King'.

Even during their league careers, when they have become established, there are a number of ways in which strikers can suddenly appear to have reinvented themselves. One of the most unusual success stories was that of Bryan 'Pop' Robson when he was at the start of his career at Newcastle in the 1960s. Though Robson did well in his first two or three seasons at St James's Park, the problem for him was that he was torn between football and golf. He devoted so much time to the latter that it took the edge off his sharpness in goalscoring situations.

Robson became so 'slow off the mark' that Newcastle were considering putting him on the transfer list. But Robson then came into contact with a man called Len Heppell, a local nightclub owner, a former professional dancing champion and an expert on body movement and balance in relation to sport. Heppell worked with a number of top players, including Peter Shilton and Bobby Moore, but he paid particular attention to Robson. After all, Robson was dating Heppell's daughter, Maureen, one of the top table-tennis players in the country who was to become the striker's wife. So for his father-in-law-to-be, the quest to make Robson quicker became virtually a personal crusade.

Throughout the close season, Robson was subjected to an intensive programme of exercises designed to change his posture, running gait and step patterns. 'When I went to his house, I had to practise running up the stairs lightly,' he recalled. 'I had to do it lightly enough for him not to hear me. It was a bit nerve-racking – he had two big Alsatians at the time.' Another aspect of his training under Heppell was that he had to play table tennis for two to three hours each day. The results of this were plain for all to see the following season, not to mention the rest of Robson's 21-year career as a player. The legendary ex-Newcastle striker Jackie Milburn summed it up when he approached Heppell and asked, 'What has happened to Pop? He looks like a sprinter who has had lead taken out of his boots.'

Even then, many would-be buyers would have been tempted to put him under the microscope to see if they could find anything else that might be wrong with him. To varying degrees, all signings are gambles, but it is those involving strikers that often provoke the most procrastination. As Gordon Strachan said, 'You really can tie yourself in knots when you are assessing a striker. It's good to not want to make a mistake, to do your homework properly, but I think you can take this to the extreme. Obviously, the closer you study him, the more likely it will be that you will see him do something wrong or have a bad game. You can easily take it out of context.'

'The number of goals he averages per season has to be the starting point,' Mark McGhee said. 'Some people score a lot of goals and others can't and never will. I sometimes forget this when I am organising a team to defend free-kicks and corners. They [the opposition] might have two tall guys who get involved in set-pieces, and I am telling our lads, "Right, you mark him, you mark him." Then, suddenly, I think, "Why are you doing this? They hardly ever score." As far as strikers are concerned, you will find that some play on the periphery and that these tend to be the ones who get, say, ten goals a season as opposed to twenty or twenty-five goals a season.' Still, as McGhee went on to point out, such bare statistics do not show the service the strikers have received, the standard and styles of play of their teams and the number of chances they have missed. Thus, though scoring records do not lie, they can be misleading. 'It [the terms of reference in the assessment of potential striker signings] is not easy to simplify,' McGhee added. 'What sort of striker do you need? A target man? A runner? Are you going to be able to play in a way that will bring the best out of him? If he is coming from a lower division, is he going to be able to adjust to the higher level? If he doesn't make the grade with you, will you get back what you paid for him? There are so many factors involved. I am inclined to look at the whole package in a player, but it's not unusual for me to make a decision on him based on something quite subtle or non-specific – just a gut feeling sometimes. When I was manager of Leicester, I remember going with Martin George [the club chairman] to watch Pontus Kamark [the Swedish full-back playing for IFK Gothenburg]. Early in the game he hit a pass of great quality from one side of the field to the other, and I said to Martin, "Let's go. I've seen enough." You see one small thing and that's it. It can be the same with strikers. One I wanted to sign for Millwall was Brett Ormerod [who was bought by Gordon Strachan for Southampton from Blackpool]. We had watched him a couple of times and I felt that his work-rate, enthusiasm and pace were bound to bring him goals at our level. Although his touch wasn't great, he had too many other things going for him for us to be unwilling to take a chance on him.'

If any club at Football League level have benefited from their willingness to take chances on strikers, to rely on their ability to unearth rough diamonds and polish them, it's Bristol Rovers. In recent years, the strikers they have picked up, mainly from schoolboy and non-league football, and then sold on for a profit have included Marcus Stewart, Barry Hayles, Bobby Zamora, Jamie

Cureton, Jason Roberts and Nathan Ellington. The money they paid for these six amounted to a couple of hundred thousand pounds; the money they received for them totalled more than £6.5 million. Though Rovers needed the cash to ease their financial problems, and the players inevitably wanted to move on to bigger stages, it's easy to see why their fans have had mixed feelings about the situation. After Rovers had narrowly failed to reach the Second Division promotion play-offs in 2000, Zamora, Cureton and Roberts were sold to Brighton, Reading and West Bromwich Albion respectively. The following season, Rovers were relegated; the season after that (during which they eventually sold Ellington to Wigan), they came close to losing their league status. The success of Zamora at Brighton will have been particularly painful to Rovers followers. His goals were the main reason why Brighton were able to climb from the Third Division to the First in successive seasons.

The progress of those strikers at Rovers reflected enormous credit on the hard work and expertise of their manager at the time, Ian Holloway, and his coaches Gary Penrice and Garry Thompson, especially as, according to Thompson, the trio's opinions about the players' potential was not widely endorsed by some figures at boardroom level.

In some cases, they were in good company. Take Jason Roberts, who started his career at Wolves and was signed on a free transfer by Rovers at the age of twenty, without having made any league appearances for the Molineux club. Thompson, the former Aston Villa and West Bromwich Albion centre-forward, said, 'I was with Northampton when I first saw him. He had been loaned to Torquay, and in his match against us he caused absolute havoc in our defence. He was big, strong and quick, and though he was very raw, he just struck me as a lad who was willing to learn. I asked someone who had worked with Jason for his views about him, and he said, "Oh, he's effing hopeless." The guy was particularly critical of his ability to hold the ball with his back to the goal and bring other people into the game. "He keeps falling over," he said. Well, OK, I could see where he was coming from. But I knew this aspect of his game could be improved. One thing I noticed about Jason was that he tended to receive the ball square on. If you do that, and the centre-half pushes you in the back, then unless you have the strength and the build of a Mark Hughes you are bound to be knocked off balance and lose possession. When he joined Rovers, it was just a case of him learning to take the ball side-on, so that he could see the defender and hold him off.'

West Bromwich Albion paid £2 million for Roberts in July 2000 (the only previous time Rovers had received that much for a player was when they sold Hayles to Fulham in November 1998). He didn't have the happiest of times there, but his fortunes rose again after Wigan signed him for £1.8 million in the 2003/04 season. His partnership with Nathan Ellington was one of the most effective in the First Division; but for Roberts' suspension at the tail-end of the season it could easily have propelled Wigan into the Premiership.

On the subject of rough diamonds, Southampton's Ray Clarke, the only ex-striker filling a chief scout role in the Premiership, recalled his spell at Coventry and the club's signing of the young Belgian centre-forward Cedric Roussel from Gent. 'People said that he wasn't good enough for the Premiership because he wasn't the quickest or most polished of strikers,' Clarke said. 'I don't think that his scoring record for us – about eleven goals in 31 matches – was bad. In any case, we bought him for other reasons. He was a big lad and we felt that he would be able to hold the ball up for us and give us the greater physical presence we needed to help bring out the best in players like Robbie Keane. Our most impressive performance with Cedric in the side was a 3–2 home win over Arsenal. He caused all sorts of problems for Arsenal's central defenders Tony Adams and Martin Keown. In fact, a couple of days later I got a call about it from Arsenal's chief scout. "Where did you get the boy Roussel from?" he asked. "He really battered our two central defenders and there aren't many strikers who have done that."

'Cedric wasn't with Coventry for very long, just a season. Unfortunately, apart from injuries, he had some personal problems. But he did do a job for us, and though some people felt that we ended up paying too much for him [£900,000], we did get more than £1.5 million for him when we sold him to Wolves.' What a great piece of business that proved for Coventry. Roussel failed to make an impact with Wolves, whose determination not to lose more money on him than was absolutely necessary when offloading him led to the striker taking his case to Fifa. He was eventually transferred back to Racing Genk for an 'undisclosed' fee.

Generally, it is foreign strikers who represent the biggest transfer-market gambles. In addition to the problems for them in Britain caused by the language barrier and cultural differences, Clarke pointed out, 'Teams in England tend to "hit" their front men earlier than they do in other countries. The game here is not as studious and technical. It's quicker and more competitive, and I think players have to work harder. The pressure is relentless.' Indeed, for every Henry or van Nistelrooy there are plenty of other foreign strikers who have not fared as well in England as their obvious talent promised. And in some cases, that's putting it mildly.

Southampton themselves saw that side of the coin through the extent to which Ecuador's 2002 World Cup star Agustin Delgado (effectively brought to the club by the chairman, Rupert Lowe) became conspicuous by his first-team absence. So, too, did Blackburn after buying Corrado Grabbi for £6.7 million; Middlesbrough after signing Massimo Maccarone for a club-record

£8.15 million; Aston Villa after they also broke their transfer-market spending record by splashing out £9.5 million on Juan Pablo Angel; and Liverpool following their £10 million purchase of El Hadji Diouf. At least Angel, who was signed by John Gregory, then banished to the sidelines by Gregory's successor Graham Taylor, but who finally found an ally in Taylor's successor David O'Leary, came good eventually. In the 2003/04 season, his third in English football, the Colombian became the first Villa player to score twenty goals or more in a season for eight years. Suffice it to say that in the light of his previous Villa Park record his presence among the leading Premiership scorers was one of the season's surprises. Meanwhile, Middlesbrough were still waiting for Maccarone to live up to their expectations and Blackburn gave Grabbi a free transfer. As for Diouf, Gérard Houllier admitted that the Senegalese World Cup star's poor performances were a factor in Liverpool parting company with the manager.

Of course, British strikers have also had mixed fortunes abroad. Even scorers in the class of Jimmy Greaves and Ian Rush found it an uphill struggle when they moved to Italy. Greaves lasted only four months at AC Milan, and Rush spent just a season with Juventus, where he got seven goals in 29 matches in 1987/88 before returning to his spiritual home of Liverpool.

It has been suggested that the big clubs in other countries tend to be less conservative in their transfer-market shopping for overseas players than their English counterparts. One wonders what they would make of the thoroughness with which Clarke assesses potential signings for Southampton. Clarke has initiated a system whereby every time he or one of the Southampton scouts under his jurisdiction runs the rule over a player, he has to log his evaluation of his performance on a four-page document. The one Clarke has formulated for strikers comprises eight sections, each of which is broken down into around eight aspects of their game. Alongside every one is an 'Excellent, Very Good, Good, Average, Poor' ticking box. It seems to go against McGhee's point about 'gut feeling', but, Clarke said, 'While that does come into it – it has to – I don't think you can have too much data about a player, especially if you are a Premiership club. The Premiership is a different world compared with, say, the Nationwide League. You have to be as discerning as you can because the standard is so high. As far as strikers are concerned, it's one thing to get X number of goals in the Nationwide League, quite another to get the same number in the Premiership, where defenders don't make as many mistakes.'

During the 2003/04 season, the Nationwide striker who impressed him the most was Jonathan Stead. Clarke was one of a number of Premiership scouts attracted to the 21-year-old as he emerged as one of the leading scorers in the Third Division with Huddersfield. Having been with the club since leaving school, Stead had established himself in their first team only the previous season and his scoring record then was just six goals in 42 matches. Clarke found that difficult to believe when confronted with the assessment reports he had gathered on the player's 2003/04 performances. One that was particularly complimentary to Stead concerned his performance against Doncaster Rovers in January 2004. Stead was assessed as 'very good' or 'good' on all but one of the points in his evaluation document for that game. The exception concerned his movement, for which he was deemed to have been 'excellent'. On top of this, he received a mark of eight out of ten for his overall performance and nine out of ten for his potential. As for 'gut feeling', Clarke said, 'Whenever I saw him, he always looked dangerous. I liked the fact that he was always looking to play on the shoulder of defenders – I don't like to see strikers go too short when they have the chance to get in behind defenders – and he also impressed me with his football intelligence and composure. I remember a great goal he scored against Mansfield. When the ball was crossed from the right, the odds on him reaching it before the keeper could only have been 60/40, if that. But he had the presence of mind to dummy it and, with the keeper having sold himself, the finish was just a formality for him. OK, it was the Third Division, but I thought, "Yeah, and he's only twenty."'

In view of all this, one would have thought that Southampton and the other clubs interested in him would have been beating a path to Huddersfield's door, especially as the fee Huddersfield were demanding (£1.25 million plus performance – or achievement-related 'add-ons') didn't seem unreasonable. One club widely reported as having made a bid for Stead was Sunderland, but they were unwilling to match Huddersfield's asking price. Others, Southampton included, preferred to play a waiting game.

The issue, which came to a head in March, created something of a dilemma for Southampton, because of Gordon Strachan's decision not to remain their manager. Rupert Lowe, who has the final say on all transfer deals at the club, was sensitive about the possibility that, while Strachan might like Stead, his successor would take a different view of the signing. Moreover, Lowe's debate with other members of the training and coaching staff over Stead didn't produce any overwhelming conclusions about his ability one way or the other.

On top of all the usual pros and cons involved in assessments of young players in the lower divisions, Stead didn't immediately strike one as having the athleticism required of a Premiership player. At 6ft 3in and just over twelve stone, he has a gangling build that can give the impression of his lacking the power to hold off opponents and get away from them. Clarke said, 'I had an argument over this with a friend of mine who had seen him play. He asked whether I thought

Stead was quick enough for the Premiership, and I said, "Well, he's not greased lightning, but I think he's quick enough, and if he isn't quick enough now, I'm sure he will be." The way I looked at it was that he had yet to fulfil his physical and mental potential. I felt he could get stronger with the right training, and through that he would get quicker as well.

'To be honest, if it had been down to me I would probably have taken a chance on him,' Clarke admitted. 'But I wasn't about to throw my dummy out of the pram [when Blackburn bought him]. While I have confidence in my ability to judge players, I have long learnt that you cannot be too dogmatic about these things. It's all about opinions, and sometimes, what might have seemed the wrong opinion in hindsight might still have been the right one at the time. Yes, I think Stead has the potential to be a good Premiership player, but with respect to him, we aren't talking about an Henry or a van Nistelrooy. I am quite aware of how I could be proved wrong about him.'

Blackburn, of course, needed to take that Stead gamble more than Southampton did. They were in danger of being relegated at the time, and with Grabbi having failed to adjust to English football and Andrew Cole and Dwight Yorke not performing as they had at Manchester United, they badly needed some fresh firepower to get them out of trouble. Stead responded to the challenge impressively, scoring five goals in his opening ten matches – goals that directly brought them thirteen points from those games – and prompted increasingly flattering public comments about his performances from Blackburn manager Graeme Souness. After Stead's second goal in as many matches in the 1–1 draw against Newcastle, Souness said, 'The way he took it was reminiscent of Alan Shearer. It was a really aggressive finish. Jon was going to make sure that the ball was only going to finish up in one place – in the back of the net. He pleased me in other ways. He embarrasses people with the amount of honest running he does for himself and the team, and if you do that you have a chance of being a player.' After his tenth goal, in the 1–0 win at Everton, Souness added, 'Every week I try to play down Jon's contribution, but sooner or later I'm going to have to tell the truth.' Perhaps one newspaper summed it up best when referring to Stead's part in Blackburn's improved results as a 'one-man rescue act'.

'I'm pleased for the lad,' Clarke said. 'But the biggest test for him will be in maintaining his form. That's another point that comes into the equation when you are assessing the ability of young strikers. When a lad first comes into a team, it's not unusual for him to do well initially. He's playing on adrenalin, on naivety if you like. But what happens when that burst of excitement has worn off and opposing teams have become more aware of what he has to offer? How is he going to handle the pressure of people expecting him to do well as opposed to hoping he will do so? I would say that strikers – goalscorers – tend to experience the biggest problems in these areas. You look at the attention Wayne Rooney has attracted. For all his brilliance, it's going to be difficult for him to cope with all the expectations that have been heaped on him.'

Still, Stead, in his bid to keep progressing, has no shortage of role models. One to have made it as a top Premiership striker after initially catching the eye at the bottom of the Football League ladder is Dion Dublin. After being released by Norwich City (without making any first-team appearances) and then going into non-league football with King's Lynn, Dublin was a member of the Cambridge United team that rose from the old Fourth Division to the Second in successive seasons in the early 1990s. He became a top-flight player with Manchester United, and maintained his status with Coventry (where he gained his England caps) and, most recently, Aston Villa.

'I have never been the quickest player in the world,' he said, 'but I was always good in the air, my touch was good and I had a hunger for goals.' Cambridge, under the management of John Beck, were hardly among the most stylish of teams. Dublin, referring to Beck's adherence to a no-frills long-ball game, admitted, 'In a way, I was possibly a better player than I might have looked there. We were a young team, and we knew we could play, but it [Cambridge's pragmatic style] was working, so who were we to argue with the manager? Also, I was learning all the time. In training, John Beck and Chris Turner [his assistant] gave me countless coaching tips in connection with my movement in the box and things like that, and I just got better and better. I also had some great advice from people like Brian Kidd at Manchester United and Gordon Strachan at Coventry.

'The fact is that I have always been able to take all the coaching tips on board and never ever felt that I had nothing more to learn. I think the real secret of being able to adjust to different levels is having a good football brain. The higher you go, the more important it becomes for you to be able to think one or two moves ahead. It's also important to be able to accept criticism. I look upon myself as an "old-school" striker because, no matter how much success I might have achieved, I don't want to be mollycoddled. Obviously I don't want my manager or coach to be rude or disrespectful to me, but I like to be told if I haven't done something well or not had a good game, and I like him to explain why.'

It probably goes without saying that, to Clarke, even better role models for Stead (and any other young striker on the way up) are Shearer, Henry and van Nistelrooy. Clarke is particularly enamoured with the latter. Having long felt a particular affinity with Dutch football through his background as a player in Holland and his contacts in the country, Clarke was among the first English football figures to recognise that van Nistelrooy could become an outstanding player. Clarke had started keeping tabs on the Dutchman at the end of the 1996/97 season, when the player was just twenty and playing mainly as an attacking midfielder for Den Bosch in the Dutch Second Division. Clarke was Southampton's reserve-team coach then and, with his team's fixtures completed, had gone to Holland for a week or so to watch some matches there. The following season, by which time Clarke had been brought to Coventry City by Gordon Strachan as the club's European scout, van Nistelrooy had made a step up the ladder in Holland with a move to Heerenveen.

Heerenveen isn't among the leading clubs in Holland, but any doubts Clarke might have had about van Nistelrooy being able to get to the top were finally dispelled when he watched him make his debut as a substitute for Holland's under-21 team, and then score twice for Heerenveen in 4–2 win over Utrecht the following Saturday. Clarke recalled, 'I said to Gordon, "This guy is going to be a top player." Alex Miller [Coventry's assistant manager] then went to watch him, and finally Gordon did so as well. I'm not sure if either was as excited about him as I was – don't forget, I had watched him a number of times – but both agreed that he had a lot of potential.'

That Coventry did not take their interest in van Nistelrooy further was due partly to the fact that Heerenveen, who had paid only £400,000 for van Nistelrooy, said that they wanted at least £4 million for him (his eventual transfer fee when he moved to PSV Eindhoven in 1998 was £4.2 million, a record deal between Dutch clubs). Moreover, it coincided with Coventry's existing first-choice strikers, Dublin and Darren Huckerby, coming to the fore and establishing one of the hottest scoring partnerships in the Premiership. 'Coventry were not a club who could afford to pay that sort of money for any player and put him on the bench,' Clarke said.

'You also had to take into account that van Nistelrooy had reached a stage in his career where he was looking beyond clubs such as Coventry. PSV Eindhoven are one of the biggest and most successful clubs in Holland, but Coventry, despite being in the Premiership, were not one of the biggest and most successful clubs in England.

'Because of my connections with Dutch football, I started receiving calls from friends of mine at other clubs asking for advice on him,' he added. 'There was a feeling that he did not work hard enough and was a bit of a prima donna. However, as Coventry weren't going to try and sign him I saw no reason not to tell them exactly what I felt about him. I just said, "Go and get him."'

This became increasingly a case of stating the obvious. In his first season with Eindhoven, van Nistelrooy was the top scorer in the Dutch League with 31 goals in 34 matches, which put him in second place in the European Golden Boot rankings, and was voted the country's Player of the Year by his fellow professionals. The following season it was 29 goals in 23 matches. No club needed convincing that he was a special talent by this stage, least of all Manchester United. Their first attempt to sign him, for £19 million towards the end of the 1999/2000 season, floundered because of medical worries concerning a previous knee injury. But even after those fears had been brought into sharp focus shortly afterwards by the torn cruciate ligament that was to force him out of action for the best part of a year, United were unwilling to give up on him.

In his first season at Old Trafford, he became the first player in United's history to score in seven successive matches (a sequence that was stretched to eight matches), and his eventual total of 36 in all competitions was the best by a United player for fourteen years. He again pushed Henry into second place the following season, with 44. It was a different story in the 2003/04 campaign, although fans of van Nistelrooy will be quick to point out that he was playing in a revamped, comparatively unsettled team.

In September 2003, Ron Atkinson, in his column in the *Guardian*, wrote, 'There has been a change in the way Manchester United play since David Beckham and Juan Sebastian Veron left. Without them they do not have the same invention in their passing, and that is particularly noticeable when Paul Scholes is injured. Instead of opening up teams with their passing, they are looking more to Cristiano Ronaldo and Ryan Giggs to run at people. The difference is obvious in the runs Ruud van Nistelrooy is making. With Beckham and Veron around, he would often spin off his marker and spring on to clever balls played behind the defence. Now the passing tends to be safe bread-and-butter stuff and he is getting a lot of possession to feet with his back to the goal.' For all this, his record was still good enough to put him in the number two spot on the Premiership's scoring list; and of course unlike Henry, he was among the leading European Championship scorers. Indeed, he is more than Manchester United's top scorer. He is also their most saleable playing asset.

Is there anything van Nistelrooy lacks as a striker? 'My only criticism of him would be that he is not physical enough,' Clarke said. 'With the greatest of respect, though he is a big lad [6ft 2in, 12st 13lb], he doesn't use his physical power as much as I feel he could.' Then he smiled, and added, 'But maybe he doesn't need to because he has so much.'

CHAPTER TEN
THE GREATEST GOALS

'Quite often it's the younger players,
the players who are relatively
free of inhibitions, who are the
most adventurous.'

TREVOR FRANCIS

THE GREATEST GOALS

Goals are generally remembered long after other aspects of a match have been forgotten. But of all the shots and headers that have found the net in top-level football since the war, and especially those seen by big television audiences, which have been the best?

Such questions can always be relied upon to spark a long, animated debate among followers of the game. There are, of course, a number of ways in which the merits of various goals can be assessed, as Trevor Francis acknowledged when we discussed the ones that have tended to be featured prominently in books and videos on the subject. 'You have to be very specific in your criteria,' Francis pointed out, 'and even then it can be extremely subjective. I have lost count of the number of goals that have excited me and I would find it very difficult to narrow them down to what I would consider to be my biggest favourites. Where do you draw the line?'

A goal doesn't necessarily need to come across as technically spectacular to stand out in the memory. If one is talking about important goals, there are, for example, those scored by Adrian Heath and Mark Robins for Everton and Manchester United respectively. Both were typical 'bread-and-butter' striker goals, apparently simple, straightforward efforts that illustrated some of the fundamental requirements of the front man's job rather than outstanding individualism. However, those goals will always be recognised as major defining moments in the histories of the two clubs.

Heath's strike came during Everton's fifth-round League Cup tie against Oxford United at the Manor Ground in January 1984, at a time when Everton were near the bottom of the First Division and there was much speculation about the future of their manager, Howard Kendall. Having been appointed in 1981, Kendall had struggled to improve the team's fortunes and it was widely believed that defeat against Oxford, then at the top of the Third Division, would signal his departure. Few would have bet against that defeat occurring after Bobby McDonald gave the home team the lead. But nine minutes from the end Heath got the equaliser. There didn't look to be much for Oxford's fans to worry about when defender Kevin Brock gained possession and, under pressure from Peter Reid, elected to play the ball back to his keeper. But the pass was under-hit, and because of Heath's anticipation and predatory instincts, Oxford were unable to get away with it. Heath, clean through with only the keeper to beat, was the epitome of coolness as he applied the finishing touch. From that day on, Kendall and Everton went from strength to strength. Everton beat Oxford 4–1 in the replay and went on to reach the final, where they lost to Liverpool. They also reached the FA Cup final, this time ending up victorious (against Watford), and finished seventh in the league. Over the next three seasons they won the championship twice, the European Cup Winners' Cup, and reached another two FA Cup finals.

Robins' goal, in a 1–0 FA Cup third-round win at Nottingham Forest in January 1990, was an even more famous turning point in football, for Alex Ferguson at Manchester United. As with Kendall at Everton, Ferguson had been at United for three years and had failed to produce the results and performances expected of him. United had slipped since the heady days of their European Cup triumph in 1968 (the last time they had qualified for the competition through being champions), and their decline was such that in 1990 their chairman and major shareholder, Martin Edwards, had come close to selling his controlling interest in the club to Michael Knighton. When United turned up to play Forest, they were fifteenth in the table and had gone eight matches without a win; their first-choice strikers Mark Hughes and Brian McClair were going though a lean period and United had scored no more than three goals in that period. A few months earlier they had been walloped 5–1 at Manchester City; and when they were beaten at home by Crystal Palace in December 1989, on the third anniversary of Ferguson's arrival from Aberdeen, a banner unfurled at Old Trafford's Scoreboard End read: 'Three years of excuses and it's still crap. Ta-ra Fergie.'

In the week of the Forest match, the consensus of media opinion about Fergie's position was that he was living on borrowed time and that an early exit from the FA Cup – by that stage the only competition he could win – would mean time-up for him at Old Trafford.

As for Robins, he was only twenty and was making only his third full first-team appearance. Ferguson had described him as 'the best finisher at the club', which was borne out to some extent by Robins' scoring record for the reserves, but the manager felt that he had a long way to go to become a serious contender for a regular place in the side at the expense of Hughes or McClair. Apart from his comparative lack of experience, there were also reservations about Robins on the grounds of his limited overall contribution to his teams. He himself drew attention to this after he had left United when he was asked to comment on United's signing of Andy Cole, a striker who seemed no less focused than Robins had been on getting on the end of attacking moves. 'I'm quite happy now to be talked of in those terms, and I'm sure Andy Cole is too,' Robins said. 'People say, "All he does is score goals," but that seems a pretty good label to me. My all-round game has actually improved a lot. At Norwich [his second club] I concentrated more on my contribution outside the box, which affected my goal ratio but made me a better team man. Now [at Leicester] I want to get back to what I'm good at.'

The chance to do what he was good at for United against Forest stemmed mainly from the injuries that rendered a number of their key players unavailable for selection. Among them was the club captain, Bryan Robson, whose place in midfield was filled by McClair, with Robins brought in to fill the latter's role as Hughes's partner up front. In a tight, scrappy match, Hughes and Robins combined to bring United the only goal after 55 minutes. The move began with United's Lee Martin dispossessing Thorvaidur Orlygsson near the left touchline; he just managed to stop the ball going out of play and then played a short pass to Hughes. The Forest defence was caught square as Hughes curled the ball into the goalmouth with the outside of his right foot, and Robins, having made a cleverly timed run to get in front of the last defender, Stuart Pearce, did the rest. It was hardly a 'Roy of the Rovers' type of goal; the ball bounced up invitingly as Robins got the better of the Forest and England left-back, and he was able to find the net with a gentle stooping header. But thanks to missed chances by Forest's striker Nigel Jemson, United held on to that lead – and Ferguson held on to his job.

It proved, of course, to be the launching pad for United to win the FA Cup that season – their first trophy for five years – for Ferguson to establish himself as the most successful manager in

British football history, and for Manchester United to become the world's richest club. Robins' fate was rather different. Though he scored decisive goals in other FA Cup rounds that season, against Newcastle in the fifth round and Oldham in the semi-final replay, he was on the substitutes bench for both United's matches against Crystal Palace in the final. He was sold to Norwich two years later and his career, punctuated at one time by tabloid reports about his turbulent private life, continued to follow a less glamorous and successful path than many might have anticipated. Still, Robins, a Sheffield Wednesday player in the 2003/04 season, has inevitably remained a difficult player to ignore for the hordes who follow Manchester United. Even now, whenever he comes into contact with a United fan, anywhere, he is liable to have his hand shaked. One suspects that in the company of a United follower he will never have to buy a drink.

And imagine the celebrity status Robins would have achieved had that goal against Forest been in the class of the ones that can be seen in most of those 'Great Goal' videos, the sort that immediately spring to mind when one thinks of the truly great players: Puskas, Pele, Carlos Alberto, Maradona, Van Basten, Beckham . . .

It's a potentially endless subject, but how's this for a short-list to sate the appetites of all goal gluttons?

FERENC PUSKAS: Hungary's third goal in the 6–3 win over England at Wembley in November 1953.

England captain Billy Wright can never have had a more embarrassing experience throughout his 105-match international career than the one Puskas inflicted upon him when a cross landed at the roly-poly Hungarian's feet on the edge of the six-yard box.

That was more than enough to give Puskas a great scoring chance, but he made it even better as Wright attempted a last-ditch sliding tackle. Wright was left tackling thin air because as he lunged in, Puskas pulled the ball away from him with the sole of his left foot. It was a drag-back par excellence, and the next step – a searing shot past the keeper, also with that magic wand of a left foot – was a formality. 'What struck me about this goal,' said Trevor Francis, 'apart from the dexterity with which Puskas beat Wright, was the extent to which he wanted to use his left foot. Most players who favour one side as much as he did can be described as being too predictable. But the only thing predictable about this goal was that it was predictably brilliant. A lot of players would have felt they had a reasonable chance of scoring without having to do that trick. Puskas did not have a bad shooting angle for a finish with the right foot when the ball came over to him; one touch, if that, and a sidefoot might have done it. But Puskas clearly had it in mind to get a lot of power into the shot, on the premise that even if the keeper got to the ball he would be unlikely to keep it out, and for him, getting the ball on to that left foot was the best way to achieve this. When Wright put him under pressure, Puskas's quickness of thought, confidence and composure were tremendous.'

PELE: Brazil's third goal in the 5–2 win over Sweden in the 1958 World Cup final.

What a way for the then seventeen-year-old Pele to mark his arrival on the World Cup stage. He had already scored the only goal in the 1–0 win over Wales in the quarter-final – on his debut – and a hat-trick in the 5–2 victory against France in the semi-final. He got two more against Sweden, one with a leap for a cross and a header that made it difficult to believe that, at 5ft 8in, he was considerably shorter than the defenders he beat. But his other goal, his first, was the one that made the biggest impact. From a Nilton Santos pass, Pele edged the ball past one defender with his chest and then, most memorably, he coolly hooked the ball over the head of another. His next touch was to despatch it into the net on the volley. 'People in the game all acknowledge the importance of a player's first touch,' said Francis, 'especially if he is a striker working in tight areas inside the box. If that's not right, then whatever ability you might have as a finisher is bound to be undermined. That's why the aspect of this goal which probably made the biggest impression on me was the way in which Pele, off the ground, controlled the ball away from the first defender with his chest. Players need to be very well balanced to achieve the mastery of the ball that Pele showed in that situation. It set him up perfectly for what was to follow. Apart from anything else, that goal also showed the determination and single-mindedness that scorers need. He was actually fouled by the next defender he beat: the player caught him at the top of his thigh, and Pele could easily have gone down and got a penalty. But there was only one thing on his mind: to keep going and put the ball in the net.'

CARLOS ALBERTO: Brazil's fourth goal in the 4–1 victory against Italy in the 1970 World Cup final.

As with Real Madrid at club level, Brazil are the national team that has traditionally put the biggest emphasis on open, attacking football. Their reputation for playing without inhibitions, with all players expressing their creative talents and making themselves potential scorers no matter what their positions, was summed up perfectly by that Alberto goal. The wonderful build-up to it started just outside the Brazil penalty area and comprised eight passes and a mazy Clodoaldo dribble through four Italian defenders. For the last phase of the move, Rivelino, on the left flank, hit the ball down the line to Jairzinho, who moved inside and squared it to the feet of Pele in the middle. Pele's path to goal was blocked by Italy's captain and sweeper Giacinto Facchetti, who also had a team-mate covering him. But Pele knew that he would not have to wait very long for support. Within seconds, Alberto, making a late run into the area to Pele's right, was alongside him. Pele knocked a simple pass into his path, and the Brazil right-back and captain did the rest with a thunderous low shot across the keeper. 'This was what I would describe as the best "team" goal I have seen,' said Francis. 'One of the things it highlighted was Pele's ability to involve himself in the general play. Quite apart from the way he set up Alberto, he was involved in the early build-up deep inside his own half. The fact that he then had to get to the other end of the field as quickly as possible was no problem to him. Among the most common aspects of successful teams is that all the players want the ball – nobody hides – and that the communication among them is good. Looking at the video of this goal, I am 99.9 per cent sure that Pele got a call from Alberto as the defender was coming through behind him. It was a response to what he heard, not what he could see; and in that respect, the pass that Pele gave him is also worthy of special mention. People might say, "Oh, what was so great about a simple pass like that?" It was great because it was absolutely perfectly weighted: Alberto did not have to break stride to make the most of it. As for the finish, Alberto did what managers and coaches advise all strikers to do in that position: shoot across the keeper. Any striker in the world would be proud to produce a shot like that.'

DIEGO MARADONA: Argentina's second goal in the 2–1 win over England in the 1986 World Cup quarter-final.

Was this the greatest ever solo goal? From deep within his own half, Maradona burst through the England team with the ball before applying the coup de grâce from close range. It began with a drag-back that helped him spin away from Peter Reid and Peter Beardsley; and as he gathered momentum, his short, muscular legs pumping like engine pistons, Terry Butcher and Terry Fenwick became the next England players to find themselves trailing in his wake. Finally, it was the turn of the keeper, Peter Shilton, Maradona steering the ball wide of him as he came out to narrow the Argentinian's shooting angle and slipping it into the net with an imperiously nonchalant prod as Butcher, tearing after him for a second opportunity to stop him, was poised to get in a tackle. Earlier, of course, Maradona had greatly undermined his image, and that of the game, through the blatant cheating with which he put Argentina ahead with that 'Hand of God' goal. But the second was unquestionably thrilling enough to at least partly make up for it. 'Other memorable goals in this mould have included the one that John Barnes scored for England [in the June 1984 friendly against Brazil in Rio] and Ryan Giggs's goal for Manchester United [in the April 1999 FA Cup semi-final replay against Arsenal at Villa Park],' pointed out Francis. 'They were fantastic; from a technical viewpoint, both can be compared with Maradona's effort. But, rightly or wrongly, I always base my assessment of goals partly on the sort of matches in which they were scored, so I have to put Maradona's at the top of the list for that reason alone. Also, I don't think I have ever seen a player keep the ball under such close control while running with it at such high speed. The ball seemed to be tied to him. It was almost as if it was part of his body. The awareness he showed with his finish, in terms of his decision to take the ball past Shilton and the fact that Butcher was probably no more than a split-second away from getting in a decisive tackle, was spot on too.'

MARCO VAN BASTEN: Holland's second goal in the 2–0 win over the USSR in the 1988 European Championship final.

Volleys are the most difficult shots to execute, which is why the superb one with which Zinedine Zidane gave Real Madrid their 2–1 victory over Bayer Leverkusen in the 2002 Champions League final has gone down as one of the best finishes in the competition's history. But even that effort was not as eye-catching as the volleyed goal scored by Van Basten, the greatest centre-forward of his generation, which helped bring Holland their only major trophy. It came from a great left-wing cross by Arnold Muhren that cleared the USSR defence and picked out Van Basten on the far side of the penalty area. Even then, the USSR could not have envisaged what was to follow because Van Basten, with his marker still only a yard or two away from him, had the most difficult of shooting angles. However, as the ball dropped, Van Basten elected to hit it first time, and propelled it into the far top corner of the net. Not for nothing was Van Basten the boyhood idol of Ruud van Nistelrooy. The latter was only twelve when he saw his hero score that goal (Van Basten's twelfth of the competition). 'It was one of my most inspiring experiences,' he has said. 'I was at that match,' said Francis, 'and the goal made a big impression on me as well. I have never seen a goal quite like that; for me, only a world-class striker with an abundance of confidence in his ability would have even dreamt of trying such a shot. The fact that he pulled away from his marker as the ball came across made the shot even more difficult. He was about twenty yards from goal and the shooting angle looked virtually impossible. The defender opposing him had every right to think that he would have to bring the ball down and take him on. The keeper wasn't in a bad position, but because of the power and accuracy of the shot, no keeper in the world would have got to it.'

DAVID BECKHAM: Manchester United's third goal in the 3–0 win over Wimbledon in August 1996.

This was the goal that first brought Beckham to the public's attention. It came towards the end of the game, when United were coasting and happy just to retain possession. But Beckham, receiving the ball some 55 yards from the Wimbledon goal and noting that their keeper Neil Sullivan was off his line, had other ideas. Like a golfer playing a shot from the fairway to the green, he chipped the ball over Sullivan's head and into the net. Beckham did what even the great Pele had failed to do in the 1970 World Cup finals, when from just inside his own half, the Brazilian produced a similarly outrageous chip over the Czechoslovakian keeper, but the ball bounced narrowly wide. 'This might seem a strange thing to say,' said Francis, 'but not all professional players have enough strength in their quadriceps, or the necessary technique, to be able to hit the ball that far, never mind do so with any degree of accuracy. I sometimes watch a light-hearted Saturday-morning television programme called Soccer AM in which they invite players to attempt to chip balls against the crossbar from the halfway line. Very few players are able to do it; generally, their attempts are dreadful. OK, you could argue that hitting the ball on to the bar is more difficult than getting the ball into the net. But even if you were to ask them to do what Beckham did, without a goalkeeper there, the percentage of players not being able to manage it would be considerably higher than you might think. You would certainly have to look long and hard to find any prepared to try it in a match. For me, his goal was typical of someone not just with his ability but also his inexperience. Quite often it's the younger players, the players who are relatively free of inhibitions, who are the most adventurous.'

The latest and most vivid example, of course, is Wayne Rooney, England's star in the European Championship in Portugal. 'In terms of performing without fear, he played like Michael Owen played in the 1998 World Cup finals,' Francis said. 'But in another sense, he also played as if he had been a top player for 10 years. What i find so remarkable about Rooney is that his individualism is combined with an excellent understanding of the game. He does the right thing at the right times, which is unusual for a lad of his age.' Rooney's image as a player who can score the sort of goals that a lot of other forwards can only dream about was born publicly in October 2002, when the Everton teenager, five days before his 17th birthday, was brought on as a substitute at home against Arsenal. It was only his tenth Everton appearance but with the highlights of the match shown on ITV that night, Rooney made it one for millions to remember by running the Gunners' defence ragged and finally producing a superb last-minute lob over keeper David Seaman from 35 yards to give Everton a 2-1 win.

Great goals were very much a feature of Francis's performances when he was a teenager. Quite apart from the ones he got with long-range shots, Francis – like Rooney a first team league player when he was only 16 – recalled: 'There were a number where I collected the ball on the half-way line and dribbled past three or four defenders before scoring.'

I did not have the courage to ask Francis whether he viewed such experiences as being better than sex; publicly, it is not known whether the likes of Adrian Heath, Mark Robins, Ferenc Puskas, Pele, Carlos Alberto, Diego Maradona, Marco Van Basten and Beckham have ever subscribed to that view. But if the answer is yes, who could blame them?

INDEX

INDEX

235